# The Art of
# Italian Cooking

*by Maria Lo Pinto*
*and Milo Miloradovich*

For Gabrielle

As she embarks
on her working
life !!!

2009

love
Mama

Enjoy — Bo Rose

## *In Appreciation*

MY DEEP APPRECIATION GOES TO MY SISTERS FRANCES, Sophie, Josephine, and Rose for their inspiring encouragement and assistance in preparing and checking these recipes used by our mother and grandmother: "Nonni."

Special thanks are given my aunts, Lena Occhipinti, Fanny Di Peri, Tessie Lupo, Sophie Natoli, Concetta Barbara, Cousin Mary Terranova, and cousins Mario and Dan; and to "Mama" Bonaccolto and Uncle Vincent for their loving interest and warm generosity in contributing special family recipes.

MARIA LO PINTO

# *Foreword*

AT HOME, THERE WERE ALWAYS SIXTEEN OR EIGHTEEN persons seated at table. It was never necessary to warn the cook, hours ahead of time, that a member of the family was bringing a guest to dinner. Invariably there was sufficient food for one or two additional persons. In fact, the unexpected guest became almost a tradition in our household.

The enthusiastic appreciation of our guests and the unstinting praise of our intimate friends inspired this special book. Over and over they would exclaim and ask: "How do you cook that?" or: "What ingredients did you use to make this so palatably light and delicious?"

These repeated questions and praise made all of us ponder the great treasure of recipes that was ours. Many had been in the family for generations and had seldom, if ever, been made known outside Nonni's kitchen.

These suggestions and directions have been prepared for all those persons who pride themselves in serving the "out of the ordinary" in food. It may be just one unusual recipe for which you are searching, or it may be an entire meal that appeals to your desire to experiment with and serve new and unusual food. Whatever your cooking inclinations may be, this book is arranged in the sequence of a complete menu, making it easy to plan unique combinations. You may select a single favorite recipe from each section, beginning with antipasto and ending with *caffe espresso* (black coffe), and find you have planned your own individual menu.

Don't fear "trying out" something different for your family and friends. All good cooking—whether it be French, American, Spanish, or Italian—requires that extra bit of "liking," a little experimenting with the exact amount of "salt to taste." The good cook learns through experience that some vegetables taste better with slightly more salt, some with a little less.

It is just the same with these recipes. After using them once or twice you will begin to sense the exact quantity of seasoning that suits your family's palate. In other words, with a reasonable degree of patience you can bring out the rare and pungent flavors of the many combinations suggested in this collection. Your reward will be satisfying and, more than this, it will be unusual, for Italian food, carefully prepared, is just that.

This book is dedicated to you—to all of you who enjoy and appreciate the unusual in unusual food.

MARIA LO PINTO

# Contents

# Introduction

*Eat thy bread with joy, and
drink thy wine with a merry heart.*

ECCLESIASTES IX:7

# CHAPTER ONE

# Nonni's Kitchen

OIL—HERBS—CHEESE—PASTA

SAVORY, SPICY AROMAS FILLED EVERY CORNER OF THE LOWER floor at Nonni's. Without a doubt, Grandmother, whom we all affectionately called "Nonni," was cooking one of her special sauces. Her kitchen was a wonderland to us, and when we behaved ourselves Nonni would let us watch her blend the oils and herbs that made her sauces better than anyone else's in all the world.

The red coals were usually smoldering in the large gray fieldstone oven which occupied one corner of Nonni's spacious kitchen in her home in Marineo, a little village near Palermo. We had always been interested in that room —ever since we were big enough to toddle in to ask Nonni for hot cookies or some tasty little tidbits to nibble. The huge oven intrigued us, and we loved to watch Nonni or the cook open the center baking compartment of the triangular top which formed a chimney. When this happened, we knew there was something delicious about to be taken out and tasted.

A large stone extension formed the top of the stove and had an open grate over the center where meats were broiled. Usually there was a shiny copper pan or two standing to one side or back of the grate. It would be filled with simmering tomato or clam sauce. We learned then that the longer and more slowly a sauce simmered the better its flavor.

The lower part of the spacious oven or stove was used as a storage place for both wood and coal. We often used to bring in twigs from the nearby woodland and pack them in systematic rows beside the coal, so that Nonni's supply was never low. Our reward was a handful of *pignoli* (pine nuts) or an extra cookie.

The kitchen was at least twenty-four feet square with a bright red tile floor bordered in gay yellow, orange, and green. The sunlight streaming in through the two huge windows and open doorway revealed walls and a beamed ceiling that were snowy white.

Terra-cotta and clay casseroles, used for baking *lasagne imbottite* (stuffed noodles) or for marinating game and fish, were standing in neat rows on wooden shelves along one wall. On the opposite wall, large and small copper pots and pans hung in neat rows, awaiting the eager and expert hands of Nonni or the cook. Nonni not only loved to choose just the right pan for each special dish, but she knew how important that choice could be to the ultimate success of her cooking.

Alongside this bright display were long-handled wooden forks and spoons, in addition to copper ones of various sizes and shapes. They were all within easy reach for this dainty little woman who insisted upon doing most of the cooking herself. Though the cook was always busy, it was Nonni who supervised the special preparations and planned all the meals.

Old Italian kitchen cabinets lined the other wall. One held the smaller kitchen utensils and china and the other was filled with kitchen linens and glassware.

Water and wine jugs made of terra cotta stood on two small tables. Each one would have made a beautiful study in still life. The water jugs were more than mere decorations. They were a necessity, because in those years Nonni had none of the conveniences of our modern kitchens. All the water had to be carried from the family wells, which were about two city blocks distant. There was a small cement outlet or drain in the kitchen floor which carried away all the waste.

We loved the massive hand-hewn walnut table which stood at the other end of the kitchen. Sixteen or more of us could enjoy the gaiety of an evening meal in the warm informality of Nonni's company whenever we wished. The brightly lighted brass lamps and the candles burning in the shining copper or majolica candlesticks lent a decorative air to the whole place. The memory of the warm joy of those long evening meals—really almost parties to us—fills us with nostalgia whenever we talk about them.

We see again the picturesque setting, lighted by the old lamp and the burning candles. They often flickered out before we reluctantly left to go to our own rooms. We smell once more the delicious aroma of Nonni's pungent sauces and wonder what it was that made all her cooking so different. Was it only her skillful blending of oils and herbs, or was it her loving and careful preparation?

OLIVE OIL

Olive oil and herbs are used in practically every Italian recipe. However, in northern Italy many cooks prefer to use butter, though an extra drop of oil in this or that combination adds an indefinable distinction of flavor.

There is a legend that an olive grove, planted by the ancient Greeks and Saracens, still grows in Sicily. Though they were the first peoples to introduce the olive trees into southern Italy, it is doubtful whether any of those ancient gnarled trunks still remain.

There are two species of trees: the low gnarled type with willow-like leaves and the poplar-shaped tree, tall and slender. The olive tree is ten years old before it begins to bear the precious olive-green fruit. From then on it continues to produce for generations.

The black ripe olive is used only for eating. It is either dried in the sun and cured with salt and olive oil, or it is preserved in brine. The green species is the olive from which the oil is extracted. The crop is harvested about the middle of November. After crushing and pressing the fruit the oil is graded and distributed for home and export consumption.

The owners of large olive groves often have their own crushing and pressing machinery. The old-fashioned crusher resembles the ancient hand-operated corn press of the Philistines. It is much like the press or mill which Samson wearily turns in the opera *Samson and Delilah*. The crusher consists of a large circular vat about fifteen feet in diameter, covered by a platform on which a heavy stone wheel revolves. A long horizontal bar is attached to the wheel which crushes the olives and pits as it revolves. A patient, blindfolded little donkey is hitched to the bar, and as he walks round and round the platform, the wheel compresses the pits and olives into a conglomerate mass ready for the next process of pressing. The little animal covers several miles in his monotonous journey, and attendants often have to urge him to go on. They also watch the crushing process and continuously push the crushed mixture toward the center of the platform so that all pulp will be equally distributed and evenly crushed.

The olive pulp is then placed in large, square, porous baskets made of straw or hemp. When filled with pulp, packed ready for pressing, the baskets resemble bales of cotton. The bales are piled in tiers of six each and carefully clamped together with an iron press at the top and bottom. Each tier is then placed over a huge cement vat sunk into the ground. As the pressure of the clamps is increased, by turning an iron rod, the oil oozes down into the vats. Each vat holds about one hundred gallons of the precious liquid. When the sluggish drip-drip has finally filled the vats, the oil is ladled out layer by layer and graded.

The top layer is considered the finest quality and is called "virgin oil." The next layer is then carefully ladled out and graded. It is somewhat heavier than the first layer. This process continues until all oil has been removed and nothing is left but a dark, thick, watery residue.

Sometimes this cloudy substance is burned as a light. First it is mixed with a small amount of heavy crude olive oil and poured into a short, thick glass. Then a wick is inserted and, when lighted, produces a flame much brighter than that of an ordinary wax candle.

Should the owner of a small grove have no press of his own, there is always a public press where he may send his fruit to be crushed. His share of oil is returned to him, having been graded and measured, olive for olive. Many times the owner supplies his own containers for the family's share of oil. If no clay jars are available and he is particularly enterprising, he may slaughter and skin a goat. After the skin has been sterilized and cured, it is sewn up and used to hold the oil. The natural form is not destroyed, and when completed it looks like a small edition of a Tony Sarg balloon. The goatskin, filled with oil, closely resembles the little billy goat before his pelt became a convenient container.

While this old-fashioned crushing and pressing process still goes on in many of the small towns and villages, modern machinery has now replaced the patient little donkey.

## HERBS IN ITALIAN COOKING

A volume might easily be devoted to the history of herbs, but only those most frequently used in Italian cooking are mentioned here. The use of herbs—as the use of other seasoning—is one that grows to be highly individual. In the beginning it is good to be over-cautious and to use a smaller quantity rather than more, until you discover the subtle flavoring effect of each herb.

It is interesting to experiment with combinations of two or three different herbs. You will find that they add a "certain something" to salads as well as to cooked foods and impart a new and unusual flavor to your cookery.

The herbs included in these recipes are the favorites which made Nonni's cooking so distinctly characteristic and individual.

## HERBS

*AGLIO—Garlic:* A bulb, which has a characteristic strong scent and pungent flavor, composed of a number of smaller bulbs called cloves. Used in flavoring meats, sauces, vegetables, and salad dressings.

*ANETO—Dill:* A European herb used with its seeds for flavoring pickles. Fresh leaves sometimes used in salads.

*ANICE—Aniseed:* Sometimes called fennel seed. The aromatic seeds of a perennial plant having yellow flowers and finely divided leaves. Used in condiments, sausages, and sauce. The oil of the seed is used in flavoring pastries, and the liqueur called anisette.

*BASILICO—Basil:* A variety of sweet green leaf of delicate flavor belonging to the mountain mint species; mildly fragrant. Used in flavoring soups, stews, vegetables, fowl, meats, and sauces.

*CANNELLA—Cinnamon:* Highly aromatic bark used in powder or stick form. Used in flavoring desserts. Sometimes used in stuffings.

*CAPPERI—Capers:* Greenish flower buds of caper plant in brine. Used chiefly in salads and fish sauces.

*CHIODI DI GAROFONI—Cloves:* The dried flower bud of a myrtaceous tree. Used whole or ground as a very pungent aromatic spice in flavoring meats and game.

*CIPOLLA—Onion:* The bulb of a garden plant having a strong characteristic flavor and odor. Used quite universally in cookery.

*FOGLIE DI ALLORO—Bay Leaves:* The aromatic leaf of a shrub resembling laurel. Used in stews, sauces, and game dishes.

*MAGGIORANA—Marjoram:* The ground common sweet marjoram (a genus of aromatic mint) is very fragrant and adds a spicy flavor. Sometimes used instead of sage in sauces and stuffings.

*MENTA—Mint:* An aromatic herb of the genus *Mentha,* used in flavoring lamb, fowl, vegetables, condiments, and salad dressings.

*NOCE MOSCATA—Nutmeg:* A seed enclosed in the pear-shaped fruit of the nutmeg tree. When ground, the nutmeg is strongly fragrant. Used chiefly in desserts, and sometimes in stuffings.

*OREGANO—Orégano:* Leaves of an aromatic shrub somewhat more delicate than thyme. Used in flavoring sauces, salads, meats, and fowl.

*PEPE FORTE — Crushed Red Pepper Seeds:* Dried, crushed, hot red garden pepper with seeds.

*PREZZEMOLO—Parsley:* A European garden herb, commonly used to flavor soups, fish, stuffings, and stews; or as a garnish.

*ROSAMARINA—Rosemary:* A warm, pungent shrub with a bitter taste which changes to a delicate flavor after cooking. Generally used with veal, lamb, fish, and fowl.

*SALVIA—Sage:* A pungent, minty, grayish-green aromatic herb. Used in flavoring stuffings, meats, and fowl.

*TIMO—Thyme:* The common garden species has mild, spicy, tiny leaves. Used quite generally in soups, sauces, salads, meats, fowl, and game.

*ZAFFERANO—Saffron:* Dried orange-colored stigmas of the saffron plant. One ounce requires more than 4000 flowers. The powder is used as a mild flavoring in soups and sauces as well as for its color.

### CHEESE

Cheese, too, is used so extensively in all Italian kitchens that this list is included as a guide to assist you in becoming more familiar with the various types. All these can be easily purchased in practically every retail cheese store. You will soon become acquainted with the various mild or sharp flavors and will learn to identify the kinds used for grating and those for slicing.

*BEL PAESE:* Mild, soft, pale yellow cheese, noted for its delicacy. Round heads weigh about 5 lbs. each.

*CACIOCAVALLO:* Sicilian cheese. Yellow, hard texture; has a spicy, tangy flavor. Eaten sliced. When properly aged, may be grated for use as seasoning. Oblong loaves; about 20 inches long and 7 inches square.

*GORGONZOLA:* Very pungent, highly flavored, creamy-white, flaked with green mold, as is Roquefort cheese. Eaten sliced or crumbled for use as flavoring in salad dressings.

*INCANESTRATO:* Sicilian grating cheese (made from cow's and goat's milk combined). Used as seasoning. Very sharp and white; sometimes contains whole black pepper. Large round heads weigh about 15 to 20 lbs.

*MANTECA:* A combination of cheese and butter. The small brick of butter is covered with Mozzarella. Eaten sliced. Not a cooking cheese.

*MOZZARELLA:* A moist, smooth, white, unsalted cheese; about size of large cup. Not spicy; for use in baking as well as eating.

*MOZZARELLA - AFFUMICATA:* Smoked Mozzarella sometimes called "Scamozza." Eaten sliced only.

*PARMIGIANO:* A yellow, mild, dry cheese known as "Parmesan"; usually grated for use as seasoning.

*PECORINO:* Off-white, medium-sharp goat's-milk grating cheese. Used as seasoning.

*PROVOLONE:* Mild, rather hard-texture slicing cheese. Light yellow; molded into small balls weighing about 4 lbs. Also shaped like a large bologna weighing about 6 to 8 lbs.

*RICOTTA:* A fresh, moist, unsalted cottage cheese for cooking and pastries. Also used very much like cream cheese in sandwiches and salads.

*RICOTTA SALATA:* Salty, dry, hard ricotta; usually grated for use as seasoning. Rather mild.

*ROMANO:* Off-white grating cheese used for flavoring. Made from cow's and goat's milk combined. Sharp, tangy flavor.

*SCAMOZZA:* Smooth, white, unsalted, pear-shaped cheese; eaten sliced.

*STRACHINO:* Very sharp light yellow goat's-milk cheese; eaten sliced; never grated.

### PASTA

*Pasta—Types of Macaroni—Often Used in Italian Cooking*

"Pasta" identifies any type paste made from wheat flour. It is dried in various shapes and forms, each one of which is given a descriptive name. Pasta—in some form—is a regular part of the daily Italian menu and is served in a great variety of interesting and tempting ways. Italian grocery stores carry all types of pasta, and those most commonly used in cooking are listed here.

*ACINI DI PEPE:* Tiny pieces of round or square pasta called "pepper kernels" because they resemble them and are less than 1/32 inch in size.

*CAPPELLETTI:* Freshly prepared moist pasta shaped like "little hats"; usually filled with chopped chicken.

*CAVATONI RIGATI:* A ribbed, curved, tubular pasta about 2 inches long and ½ inch in diameter.

*CONCHIGLIE:* Pasta shaped like little sea shells. Sometimes called "maruzzelle."

*DITALI:* Pasta dried in tubular form about ¼ inch in diameter and ½ inch long.

*DITALINI:* Same shape as ditali but cut in ¼-inch lengths. Used in *minestras* and soups.

*FARFALLETTE:* A decorative pasta shaped into small and large ribbon bows. Sometimes called "butterflies."

*FUSILLI:* A spiral, curly spaghetti.

*LASAGNE:* Egg or plain noodles cut in medium and wide widths.

*LINGUINI:* Narrow, plain noodles about ⅛ inch wide.

*MAFALDE:* Long, twisted ribbon noodles.

*MEZZANI:* A smooth, curved, tubular pasta about 1 inch long and ¼ inch in diameter.

*MOSTACCIOLI:* Smooth, tubular, very hollow pasta, cut obliquely in 2½ inch lengths, about ½ inch in diameter.

*PASTINA:* Tiny pasta disks about ⅛ inch in diameter; used only in soups.

*PASTINA AL UOVO:* Shaped like pastina, but made with eggs.

*PERCIATELLI:* Long, tubular pasta; more hollow and slightly larger in diameter than spaghetti.

*RAVIOLI:* Freshly prepared, moist, very thin pasta, about 2 inches square; filled with chopped chicken, spinach, meat, or ricotta.

*RIGATONI:* Large, ribbed, tubular pasta cut into 3-inch lengths.

*SPAGHETTI:* A wheat-flour pasta dried in long, thin, tubular lengths.

*SPAGHETTINI:* Very thin spaghetti; not quite as slender as vermicelli.

*TAGLIARINI:* Very narrow egg noodles about ⅛ inch wide.

*TUBETTINI:* Tiny tubes of pasta cut into ⅛-inch lengths; used only in soups or *mine-stras.*

*VERMICELLI:* Angel hair, very thin spaghetti. Usually dried separately like spaghetti; however, sometimes 15 or 20 strands are twisted to resemble a bowknot.

*ZITI:* Plain, tubular pasta about 3 inches long and ½ inch in diameter.

# Wines, Customs, and Festivals

## WINES

IN EVERY ITALIAN HOUSEHOLD WINE TAKES THE PLACE OF drinking water. Usually a mild burgundy or chianti is served with every dinner. Drinking tart red wine is as important to the full enjoyment of eating pasta as is a good sauce.

The best chefs in the world have always used wines for flavoring, and none will deny that the correct wines, wisely served, add an indescribable charm to even the most simple meal.

Wine also has its own food value as well as flavor. Webster defines *food* as "anything that nourishes or sustains." So returning to our early lessons in nutrition, we can search for the carbohydrates and calories. Those in wine are hidden in the alcoholic content. One gram of alcohol contains more calories than an equal amount of carbohydrates, but less calories than are found in one gram of fat.

The drier red wines such as burgundy, claret, and chianti, served so often with Italian food, contain only half the calories found in the sweet wines such as port, sherry, muscatel, and tokay. If, therefore, wines are included in the menu, their actual food value should also be considered.

The proper choice of wines, as the choice of other flavoring, is something that must be acquired through patience and experience. If after experimenting you discover that your family prefers a fuller, fruitier wine than claret with spaghetti, then remember to serve chianti, zinfandel, or burgundy. There are numerous pamphlets and books from which one may learn the correct order of serving wines. Perhaps this list will be helpful to those who are just beginning to discover the many domestic wines that are plentiful and not expensive.

### CORRECT ORDER OF SERVING WINES:

| Course | Wine | Temperature |
|---|---|---|
| Antipasto | Pale dry sherry | Well chilled |
| | Old sherry | " " |
| | Dry white port | Chilled |
| | Dry vermouth | " |
| | Sweet vermouth | " |
| Oysters Shrimps | Rhine wine | " |
| Fish | Sauterne, medium or dry and haut | Well chilled |
| | Chablis | " " |
| | Riesling | " " |
| Soup | Old sherry | " " |
| | Pale dry sherry | " " |
| Spaghetti, Ravioli | Chianti | Chilled |
| Red Meats and Game | Burgundy | Chilled |
| | Claret | " |
| | Zinfandel | " |
| | Bordeaux | Well chilled |
| White Meats and Fowl | Chablis | " " |
| | Riesling | " " |
| | Rhine wine | " " |
| | Sauterne | " " |
| | Moselle | " " |
| Salad | All dry white wines | " " |
| Dessert | Sparkling burgundy | " " |
| | Champagne | " " |
| | Sparkling moselle | " " |

| Course | Wine | Temperature |
|--------|------|-------------|
| Dessert | Asti Spumanti (Italian champagne) | Well chilled |
|  | Port | Room temp. |
|  | Muscatel | "      " |
|  | Tokay | "      " |
|  | Madeira | "      " |
|  | Marsala | "      " |
| Coffee and After Dinner | Grappa | "      " |
|  | Cognac | "      " |
|  | Cointreau | "      " |
|  | Chartreuse | "      " |
|  | Crème de menthe | Frappéed |
|  | Anisette | Room temp. |
|  | Brandy | "      " |
|  | Maraschino | "      " |

## CUSTOMS AND FESTIVALS

*Capo d'Anno*———————————————————*New Year's*

Since time immemorial, festivals and feasting have been associated in the mind of man with good fellowship, good food, and much rejoicing. New Year's at Nonni's was no exception. It was usually the gayest and most elaborate celebration of all the year.

The family's best silver was brought from safekeeping. All the large serving pieces were brilliantly polished, including the lovely old coffee set and silver decanter that were Nonni's special pride. Both had belonged to her mother and, year in, year out, always occupied the center of the alabaster top of the great walnut buffet against the side wall. Tall silver candelabra, filled with softly burning white candles, stood at either end of the buffet.

This piece of furniture was more than an elaborately carved decoration. In its several large drawers, linens were kept. Wine bottles and jugs were stored in the lower compartments. A smaller corner cabinet, in which Grand-

father had ingeniously placed a wine barrel, always at-
tracted attention. It was usually filled with a favorite vin-
tage which was easily served by turning the old-fashioned
wooden spigot which protruded from the decorated barrel
head.

Two medium-sized serving tables stood near one end of
the beautiful hand-carved dining table. The twelve
matching chairs were made with rush-bottom seats. A
newcomer might have wondered at two other pieces which
completed the furnishings in the room. One was an enor-
mous couch placed against the wall and the other was an
ebony rocker which belonged to Grandfather. We of the
family knew that he often rested there after eating. We
had grown accustomed to his sitting in the rocker or even
sinking into the soft Paisley cover and downy pillows of
his couch. If he felt like it, why not? Didn't the ancient
Romans have luxurious banquet couches?

Many Italian families celebrated New Year's Eve by
serving an elaborate banquet shortly before midnight.
But at Nonni's there was Asti Spumanti with a midnight
supper. The real festivities took place on New Year's Day.
It was the time when Nonni's dining room was trans-
formed into a banquet hall with its doors swinging wide
to welcome us to the feast. The large crystal chandeliers
holding the oil lamps gleamed more brightly than ever.
Perhaps it was because the lamps had been taken down to
be trimmed and filled and the crystal washed and
polished.

The whole house was astir and excited as the pungent
aromas of specially prepared holiday food put our already
expectant appetites on edge. We knew there would be
the traditional *maialino arrostito* (roast suckling pig)
served with crackling brown *carciofi arrostiti* (roasted artichokes. The dessert for that day was always one of Nonni's
special *torta di ricotta* (Italian cheese pie) made still more
delectable by the contrasting, bitter flavor of *caffe espresso.*

The adults exchanged gifts on New Year's and there
was eating and merrymaking all day long. The dinner
often lasted well into the night, and Nonni was showered
with praise and blessings as family and departing friends
shouted again: *"Buon Capo d'Anno [Happy New Year]!"*

*Festa di San Giuseppe*————————————*St. Joseph's Day*

One of the early spring holidays with its correspond-
ingly appropriate food and special holiday menu is the
traditional St. Joseph's Day. It falls regularly on March
19. St. Joseph, the patron saint of home and family, is be-
loved by rich and poor alike. It is the tradition in Sicily
for all wealthy families to prepare huge buffets laden with
special meats, fish, pasta, fruits, vegetables, and desserts.
Then all the less fortunate neighbors are invited to enjoy
the feast.

The whole celebration begins with a religious tableau
which has been rehearsed. Villagers have been selected to
represent the Holy Family: an old man, a lovely young
woman, and a little child. The three are seated at the
head of the banquet table and remain there during the
early part of the festivity. The village priest blesses the
food, the "Holy Family" is served first by the host and
hostess, and then it is officially "open house." The priest
takes no other part in the celebration, nor does he eat
any of the food especially prepared and provided for the
guests.

All are free to come and go as they wish. The guests may
eat what they choose and as much as pleases them. The
festival lasts most of the day and well into the night. When
all have been fed, they go on their way with thankful
hearts and take the blessing of the host and hostess with
them.

It is also customary for the village officials to arrange a
public buffet in St. Joseph's honor. The banquet table invariably stands in the *piazza*—public square—opposite the
doors of the cathedral. The table is usually built around
two sides of the *piazza* in the form of a right angle. These
village tables in the public squares may not be as elaborately decorated as those in the homes, but they sag beneath the weight of choice foods and wines contributed by
the wealthy villagers. All come to this public table at
some time during the day to pay homage to the great
saint.

Many kinds of vegetable *minestras*—very thick soups—
are prepared and served at this celebration, but no cheese
is eaten on St. Joseph's Day. The spaghetti is not sprinkled

with grated Incanestrato, but in its place a traditional mixture of toasted dry bread crumbs with fresh sardines and fennel sauce is used.

Lentils, *favas*, and all types of dried beans are cooked and served with escarole and other leafy vegetables—none of which is prepared with cheese.

Then there is the special dessert without which no St. Joseph's Day buffet could ever be called by that name. It is St. Joseph's Sfinge: a large round cream puff filled with ricotta (Italian cottage cheese) and topped with red cherries and sections of glazed orange.

*Carnevale*————————————————*Carnival*

The festival known as *Carnevale* (Carnival) is the longest and gayest in the Italian calendar of annual celebrations. *Carnevale* continues the entire four weeks preceding Lent, but the latter part of the festival, called the "Two Days of the Shepherds," is the time when the whole family drops all activities to celebrate.

Food is served in great abundance and a traditional combination is *salsiccia con peperoni* (sausage with sautéed green peppers). The sausage is always broiled. Its extraordinary flavor comes from the blended seasonings of Caciocavallo cheese, chopped parsley, and fennel seed.

Everyone enters wholeheartedly into the fun of this merriest holiday of the year. There are music and dancing as young and old mingle in the public squares. Accordions, guitars, and mandolins supply the gay rhythms and lilting melodies of folk songs and ballads. Spontaneous shouts of merriment and laughter drift through the open doorways as the happy throngs of people fill the village streets.

Hilarious masquerades—similar to those of Mardi Gras —are held on the last night. At the stroke of midnight the church bells toll the beginning of Lent and all festivities cease for the forty days of fasting before Easter.

*Pasqua*————————————————*Easter*

Even breakfast on Easter Day has its traditional menu. Eggs are prepared with vegetables and varied herbs. The choice and combination depend upon the particular taste of the family. Wine and *caffe espresso* complete the morning meal.

Dinner at Easter time is perhaps the most festive one of all the year. Holiday bread, baked in many different shapes and designs, is prepared for children and grownups alike. The yellow dough is molded into dolls, baskets, and bunnies. In the center of each basket a gaily colored egg may be lodged and sometimes one is hidden under the arm of a little doll. Each member of the family is certain to receive a piece of holiday bread baked in his or her favorite design. Often Nonni used to bake a huge ring of festive bread and surround it completely with at least a dozen or more colored eggs. This decorative bread ring was placed on the Easter table as the center decoration.

Many other favorites were also prepared for us on that day. We used to have great fun watching Nonni roast the traditional *agnellino* (baby lamb). And no Easter dinner was complete without artichokes roasted to a golden brown.

For dessert there was always a great variety of cookies and nuts with spumoni. The dessert served most frequently was the one associated with the day as traditional: the tempting *cassatelli* (cream tartlets). Finally a large basket of piping-hot roasted chestnuts was placed before us; despite our satisfied feeling, we relished them with much gusto.

To give you an idea of what Nonni's Easter menu really looked like, had she written it down for you, it has been included in the list of festival menus.

*Natale————————————————————————Christmas*

Christmas Eve is ushered in with quiet solemnity and there is a traditional supper, usually served late in the evening before the family attends midnight Mass. No meat is ever eaten on that Holy Night, but in its place fish is always served. In many households it has become the custom to eat only *capitone,* a species of large thick eels. This meal is not an elaborate one and it has an air of solemn festivity. Traditional foods are included in the menu, and the soup is usually chicken broth for which *cappelletti* (little hats) have been freshly prepared. The dessert is always a rich, decorative *cassata* (cream tart).

On Christmas Day, when the children exchange gifts, there is much joy and festivity. A regular holiday feast is prepared for which each family makes up its own menu of special favorites. Invariably there are two or three rich desserts: one of these is certain to be the traditional, decorative and honeyed *pignolata-strufoli* (pine-nut clusters).

In Nonni's home at Christmas time there was always an extra-large *pignolata* placed on the buffet as an effective centerpiece. It was a great favorite with her, and for practically every celebration Nonni would also include a *cassata*. More sweets were served at Christmas than at any other time during the year, and there were *amaretti* (macaroons) and *pallottole d'aranci* (orange balls) for the children to munch as they played with their new toys.

All holidays remind us of the gay celebrations we enjoyed with Nonni. No matter where we are, when there is good food and merry music in the joyous gatherings of our family and friends, those times are forever associated in our minds and hearts with the traditions given to all of us by our loving Nonni.

CHAPTER THREE

# *Festival Menus*

IN CHAPTER TWO, "WINES, CUSTOMS, AND FESTIVALS," WE
told how most Italian holidays are occasions for gay celebrations. Naturally, menus for such days can be very unusual and highly individual.

Nonni's special menus were so characteristically hers
that several complete ones are given here.

BIRTHDAY MENU                              COMPLEANNO

*Chilled Sherry or Cocktail
Antipasto
Rice Milanese
Broiled Italian Sausage
Chicken with Orégano
Broccoli with Olives
Escarole Salad
Cream Cake de Luxe
Fruit
Nuts
Caffe Espresso
Cointreau*

Chilled claret or burgundy may be served with this
dinner. Well-chilled champagne with Cream Cake.

20

CARNIVAL MENU                                        CARNEVALE

*Cocktails*
*Antipasto*
*Gnocchi with Plain Tomato Sauce*
*Broiled Holiday Sausage*
*Sautéed Green Peppers*
*Orange and Lemon Salad*
*Torta di Pistacchio*
*Fruit*
*Caffe Espresso*
*Liqueur*

Burgundy may be served during entire meal.

CHRISTENING MENU                                        BATTESIMO

*Cocktails*
*Antipasto*
*Macaroni with Mushroom Sauce*
*Veal Rollettes*
*Roasted Suckling Pig*
*Steamed Escarole*
*Roasted Peppers*
*Lemon and Orange Salad*
*Amaretti*
*Spumoni*
*Assorted Nuts*
*Caffe Espresso*
*Champagne*
*Maraschino*

Chilled burgundy may be served with the antipasto
and roast.  Champagne with dessert.
Maraschino with coffee.

*Cocktails*
*Antipasto*
*Noodle Soup*
*Buttered Spring Chicken*
*Pan-Browned Potatoes*
*Broiled Mushrooms*
*Mixed Salad*
*Aunt Lena's Anise Slices*
*Spumoni*
*Mixed Nuts*
*Caffe Espresso*
*Brandy and Benedictine*

Chilled claret may be served with chicken. Room
temperature muscatel with the dessert.

CHRISMAS EVE SUPPER MENU              VIGILIA DI NATALE

*Vermouth with Lemon Peel*
*Antipasto*
*Cappelletti in Broth*
*Capitone*
*String Bean Salad*
*Finocchio*
*Cassata*
*Fresh Figs—Prickly Pears*
*Roasted Chestnuts*
*Caffe Espresso*
*Maraschino or Benedictine*

Meat is never served on Christmas Eve. Serve
sauterne with broth and *capitone*.
Port or tokay with *cassata*.

CHRISMAS DAY MENU                                    NATALE

*Chilled Marsala*
*Antipasto*
*Chicken Broth*
*Lasagne Imbottite*
*Italian Sausage*
*Roast Chicken*
*Fried Eggplant*
*Finocchio Salad*
*Pignolata*
*Assorted Nuts*
*Fruit*
*Caffe Espresso*
*Brandy*

Burgundy may be served during dinner. Port or
sweet herry with *pignolata*.

NEW YEAR'S EVE                     NOTTE DI CAPO D'ANNO

*Chilled Vermouth with Lemon Peel*
*Mafalde with Meat Sauce*
*Chicken with Mushrooms*
*Roasted Green Peppers*
*Tomato Salad with Orégano Dressing*
*Zabaglione*
*Fruit*
*Caffe Espresso*
*Champagne*

Well-chilled chablis may be served with chicken.

*Chilled Sherry*
*Antipasto*
*Macaroni with Plain Tomato Sauce*
*Roast Suckling Pig*
*Boiled Artichokes with Salad Dressing*
*Escarole Salad—Finocchio*
*Torta di Ricotta*
*Toasted Almonds*
*Fruit*
*Caffe Espresso*
*Anisette or Cognac*
*Asti Spumanti*

Claret or burgundy may be served with dinner.
Port, muscatel, or champagne with dessert.

TYPICAL ST. JOSEPH'S BUFFET          FESTA DI SAN GIUSEPPE

*Chilled Marsala*
*Lentil Soup*
*Spaghetti with Finocchio and Sardine Sauce*
*Roasted Artichokes*
*Italian Sausage*
*Escarole Salad*
*St. Joseph's Sfinge*
*Amaretti—Macaroons*
*Roasted Nuts—Green Almonds—Fruit*
*Caffe Espresso*
*Benedictine or Anisette*

During the entire repast, a rather tart red wine is served,
although a sweeter one may be used if preferred.

*Chilled Marsala*
*Manicotti with Tomato Sauce*
*Whole Roasted Baby Lamb*
*Sautéed Spinach*
*Roasted Artichokes*
*Mixed Salad*
*Roasted Chestnuts*
*Cassatelli*
*Fruit in Season*
*Asti Spumanti*
*Caffe Espresso*
*Cognac*

Chilled claret or riesling may be served
with baby lamb.

SPRINGTIME MENU                    PRIMAVERA

*Vermouth with Lemon Peel*
*Antipasto*
*Chicken Broth with Pastina*
*Veal with Marsala*
*Sautéed Broccoli*
*Dandelion Salad*
*Bel Paese Cheese with Toasted Crackers*
*Fruit in Season*
*Caffe Espresso*
*Anisette*

Well-chilled light dry sauterne or riesling may be
served with veal.

*Old Sherry*
*Spaghetti with Clam Sauce*
*Asparagus Parmesan*
*Chicken with Orégano*
*Romaine Salad*
*Stuffed Peaches*
*Aunt Lena's Anise Slices*
*Spumoni*
*Caffe Espresso*

Chilled claret may be served with spaghetti. A light
dry sauterne or chablis with chicken.

*Chilled Marsala*
*Antipasto*
*Minestrone*
*Brandied Duck*
*Stuffed Mushrooms*
*Cucumber and Tomato Salad*
*Apple with Gorgonzola Cheese*
*Nuts*
*Caffe Espresso*
*Cognac*

Chilled burgundy or bordeaux may be served with duck.

*Vermouth or Cocktail*
*Antipasto*
*Ravioli with Plain Tomato Sauce*
*Beef à la Mode*
*Fried Eggplant*
*Roasted Artichokes*
*Mixed Salad*
*Zabaglione*
*Fruit in Season*
*Caffe Espresso*
*Benedictine*

Chilled burgundy or zinfandel may be served
with ravioli and beef.

ANY SPECIAL WINTER HOLIDAY MENU        FESTE INVERNALE

*Chilled Marsala*
*Antipasto*
*Cappelletti in Chicken Broth*
*Roasted Pheasant*
*Rabbit Stew*
*Sautéed Mushrooms*
*Rice Croquettes*
*Mixed Salad*
*Assorted Cheeses*
*Gorgonzola, Bel Paese, Strachino, and Scamozza*
*Zuppa Inglese*
*Caffe Espresso*
*Cognac—Chartreuse*

Burgundy may be served with dinner. Cognac or
chartreuse with caffe espresso.

WEDDING MENU                           SPOSALIZIO

*Cocktails*
*Chicken Broth*
*Stuffed Noodles*
*Roasted Whole Baby Lamb*
*Roasted Artichokes*
*Mushrooms Parmesan*
*Chicory Salad*
*Cassata*
*Fruit in Season*
*Cheese*
*Caffe Espresso*
*Brandy*
*Chartreuse*

Well-chilled sauterne may be served with chicken broth.
Chianti with stuffed noodles and lamb.
Champagne with the dessert.

# CHAPTER FOUR

# *Salute!*

## DINNER BEGINS WITH ANTIPASTO

THE GLASS IS RAISED; THE TOAST IS GIVEN—*"Salute!"* (sa-looh-tay). Dinner begins with antipasto—the Italian appetizer.

The combinations served can be of individual choice, and the preparation of an attractive antipasto plate calls for much ingenuity. Its color and taste appeal depend on the variety of appetizers used as well as the manner in which they are arranged. For instance, lettuce and *finocchio* (a species of Italian celery) used as a green-and-white border will improve the appearance of even a usual selection of celery, radishes, pickled beets, salami, and *acciughe* (anchovies). If a still more colorful combination is preferred, simply add one or two large *olive nere all'olio* (Italian black olives in oil) and a strip of brilliant pimiento.

Another typical Italian variation would include *funghi con aceto e olio* (sautéed mushrooms in vinegar and oil), sliced hard-boiled eggs, *uovo di tonno* (tuna-fish roe), lettuce, and wafer-thin slices of *prosciutto* (Italian ham).

Still another appetizing combination would be *peperoncini all'aceto* (small green pickled peppers), two or three *carciofini* (artichoke hearts), a pimiento, a stalk of *finocchio, salsiccia secca* (dry pork sausage) sliced thinly, and *acciughe.*

When the choice has been made and the plate prepared, it is customary to pour olive oil and a small quantity of wine vinegar over the combination.

As one becomes familiar with antipasto one will find it fun to make up combinations to include the favorite delicacies of each individual. For instance:

*Lettuce and Sliced Tomatoes*
*Anchovies*
*Quartered Hard-boiled Eggs*
*Radishes*
*Salami*
*Celery and Ripe Olives*

OR

*Lettuce and Pickled Beets*
*Prosciutto (Italian Ham)*
*Radishes*
*Celery Hearts*
*Herring Roe*
*Green Olives*

OR

*Carciofini (Artichoke Hearts)*
*Capocollo (Sliced Smoked Pork)*
*Lettuce and Finocchio*
*Sliced Tomatoes*
*Quartered Hard-boiled Eggs*
*Peperoncini all'Aceto*
*Ripe Olives*

Usually, in most Italian households, a small glass of slightly chilled vermouth with a twist of lemon peel is served with this course. Sherry is also good if preferred.

Many of the antipasto mentioned may be purchased in Italian stores and delicatessens.

### ANTIPASTO LIST

*ACCIUGHE:* Anchovy filets.

*CAPOCOLLO:* Delicately smoked pork, sliced very thin as a salami.

*CARCIOFINI:* Artichoke hearts.

*FINOCCHIO:* An anise-flavored species of celery with

a lacy green leaf at top. Also served after dinner or in salads.

*FUNGHI CON ACETO E OLIO:* Sautéed cold mushrooms, marinated in Italian or French dressing.

*OLIVE:* Olives—green or black.

*OLIVE NERE ALL'OLIO:* Black olives cured in oil instead of brine.

*PEPERONCINI ALL'ACETO:* Small green peppers pickled in vinegar—of very tart flavor—they take the place of the American sour pickle.

*PIMIENTO:* Sweet red peppers.

*PROSCIUTTO:* Slightly pungent smoky-flavored Italian ham, served in wafer-thin slices as is salami.

*RADICI:* Radishes.

*SALAMI:* Highly seasoned Italian sausage, served in wafer-thin slices.

*SALSICCIA SECCA:* Very dry pork sausage, served in wafer-thin slices as is salami.

*SALSICCIA SECCA CON PEPERONI:* Very peppery dry sausage, served in wafer-thin slices.

*SEDANI:* Celery hearts.

*UOVO DI ARINGHE:* Herring roe.

*UOVO DI TONNO:* Tuna-fish roe.

# Recipes

# CHAPTER FIVE

# Soups

## Fish Soups

### BRODO DI PESCE CON TAGLIARINI

#### FISH BROTH WITH NARROW NOODLES

2½ lbs. whiting
¼ lb. tagliarini (narrow
  noodles)
1 large onion, sliced
1 large carrot, chopped
2 large fresh tomatoes,
  chopped

3 stalks celery
2 tbs. butter
2 tbs. olive oil
½ cup grated Parmesan
  cheese
2 qts. boiling water
Salt and pepper to taste

Have fish cleaned; leave whole; melt butter in large deep saucepan or pot; add olive oil; heat; add onion, carrot, and celery; cook over medium flame for 10 minutes; add tomatoes, salt and pepper to taste; add rapidly boiling water; cover. Cook slowly for 30 minutes. Add fish; boil slowly for 15 minutes. Remove fish carefully, using a spatula to prevent breaking. Set aside; keep hot by placing platter over steaming water.

Strain broth through colander. Bring to a boil; add tagliarini (noodles); cook 12 minutes or until tender. Serve broth very hot and sprinkle generously with grated Parmesan.

Serve fish separately with green salad and lemon slices. Serves 4 to 6.

# Meat Soups

## BRODO DI MANZO

### BEEF BROTH

| | |
|---|---|
| 2 lbs. shank beef | 1 carrot |
| 1 shank bone with marrow | 1 onion |
| | 1 potato |
| 3 springs parsley | 6 qts. water |
| 1 ripe tomato | Salt and pepper to taste |

Put all ingredients in cold water. Bring to a boil. Lower flame and cook slowly for 2 hours in covered pot.

Remove meat and bone. Remove marrow from bone; add marrow to broth. Strain broth and vegetables through colander or sieve.

Use as basic beef broth or stock.

## MINESTRONE MILANESE

### MINESTRONE MILAN STYLE

| | |
|---|---|
| ½ cup kidney beans | 2 qts. prepared soup stock |
| ½ cup rice | |
| ¼ cup olive oil | 1 sliced onion |
| 1 No. 2 can tomatoes | 1 tbs. chopped parsley |
| 1 clove garlic | 2 stalks celery, diced |
| 2 cups chopped spinach | 2 cups shredded cabbage |
| Pinch of sage | 2 cups chopped carrots |
| Salt and pepper to taste | ¼ cup grated Parmesan cheese |

Soak beans overnight. Drain.

In large pot, sauté, in hot oil, garlic, onion, and fresh vegetables for ten minutes. Stir. Add rice, beans, salt and pepper, and soup stock. Cover. Simmer until beans and rice are tender and most of soup has been absorbed.

This usually takes about 1½ hours. Add cheese and mix thoroughly.

Produces a thick, nourishing soup. Serves 6 to 8.

## NONNI'S ZUPPA DI POLLO
### NONNI'S CHICKEN SOUP

| | |
|---|---|
| 1 plump fowl (4-5 lbs.) | 3 stalks celery |
| 2 large carrots | 1 large fresh tomato |
| 1 large onion | 3 springs parsley |

*Salt and pepper to taste*

Place all ingredients in 6 quarts of cold water. Bring to a boil. Lower flame and simmer for 2 hours or until fowl is thoroughly tender and meat falls from bone. Remove fowl from pot. Strain all vegetables through a sieve. Heat exact amount for serving.

Serve piping hot and clear. Serves 8.

## ZUPPA VEGETALE CON POLPETTINI
### VEGETABLE SOUP WITH MEAT BALLS

| | |
|---|---|
| 5 qts. water | 2 stalks celery |
| 2 lbs. lean beef | 3 carrots |
| 1 veal or beef bone | 1 No. 2 can tomatoes |
| 2 large onions, halved | 3 sprigs parsley |

*Salt and pepper to taste*

Cook all these ingredients in large covered pot over low flame for 2 hours.

Strain, then add:

| | |
|---|---|
| 2 diced carrots | 3 tbs. rice |
| 2 diced potatoes | 1 cup fresh peas |

*1½ dozen small meat balls**

Boil slowly for 30 minutes in covered pot. Serve very hot. (If desired, sprinkle with grated Parmesan cheese.)

* Prepare recipe as for Polpetti (meat balls).

## ZUPPA DI SPINACI E RISO

### SPINACH SOUP WITH RICE

| | |
|---|---|
| *4 qts. water* | *3 stalks celery, diced* |
| *2 lbs. lean beef* | *1 No. 2 can tomatoes* |
| *1 veal or beef bone* | *3 diced carrots* |
| *1 large onion, halved* | *2 tbs. olive oil* |
| *1 tsp. chopped parsley* | *½ cup grated Parmesan* |
| *2 cups boiled rice* | *cheese* |
| *2 cups cooked chopped* | *Salt and pepper to taste* |
| *fresh spinach* | |

Place all ingredients except cheese, olive oil, rice, and spinach in a large pot. Cover. Cook for 2 hours over low flame.

Strain broth and vegetables.

Sauté spinach in olive oil for 2 minutes; add rice and mix. Add this mixture to broth and strained vegetables; cook 3 minutes. Serve hot with grated Parmesan cheese for added flavor. Serves 6 to 8.

Beef used for soup may be cut into small cubes when cold; add sliced onion, parsley, a little olive oil, and vinegar to taste; toss and serve with mixed green salad. Sliced tomatoes may also be placed around dish to add color and flavor.

## Vegetable Soups

## ZUPPA DI LENTICCHI #1

### LENTIL SOUP #1

| | |
|---|---|
| *1 lb. lentils* | *2 tbs. butter* |
| *3 qts. water* | *2 tbs. olive oil* |
| *1 chopped onion* | *Salt and pepper to taste* |

Wash lentils. Place in pot with cold water. Cook over medium flame about 1½ hours or until lentils are soft. Add salt and pepper.

Melt butter in separate saucepan; add oil; sauté onion for about 5 minutes or until soft and slightly brown.

When lentils are done, strain soup through sieve or colander; add onion and oil mixture; stir thoroughly. This produces a thick soup. Keep hot over low flame until served. Serve very hot. Sprinkle with grated Parmesan cheese if desired.

Serves 4 to 6.

## ZUPPA DI LENTICCHI #2

### LENTIL SOUP #2

½ lb. lentils  
1 onion  
1 clove garlic  
2 stalks celery  

4 tbs. olive oil  
1 tsp. chopped parsley  
½ cup tomatoes (stewed or canned)  

Salt and pepper to taste

Cook lentils in 2 quarts of boiling salted water for 1 hour. Chop onion, garlic, and celery; put into saucepan with oil and parsley; cook until slightly browned; add tomatoes and cook for 10 minutes longer. Pour this mixture into pot with lentils; cover; let simmer for 15 minutes or until lentils are soft.

Serve in deep soup bowls and sprinkle with grated Romano cheese if desired. Serves 4.

## MINESTRONE DI ZIO GIUSEPPE

### UNCLE JOE'S MINESTRONE

1 lb. fresh peas  
1 cup diced celery  
2 diced carrots  
1 large onion, sliced  
1 cup canned tomatoes  
½ cup olive oil  

¾ lbs. vermicelli  
3 qts. water  
½ cup grated Romano cheese  
3 diced potatoes  
Salt and pepper to taste

Clean all vegetables. In saucepan, sauté onions and potatoes in hot olive oil about 10 minutes or until medium brown. Add tomatoes, salt and pepper; cover; cook slowly about 15 minutes.

In separate pot, bring 3 quarts of water to boiling point. Add celery, peas, and carrots; cover; cook about 15 minutes or until tender. Add all sautéed vegetables and vermicelli broken into 1-inch pieces; cover; cook 20 minutes.

Serve very hot with grated Romano cheese. Serves 6 to 8.

## MINESTRONE SEMPLICE

### PLAIN MINESTRONE

½ lb. ditalini†
1 chopped onion
2 tbs. olive oil
2 cups string beans cut into small pieces
1 tsp. chopped parsley
3 qts. boiling water

2 ozs. grated Parmesan cheese
3 tbs. butter
3 stalks celery, diced
2 large potatoes, diced
1 cup fresh peas
Salt and pepper to taste

Cook onion in oil and butter about 3 minutes or until slightly brown; add celery, potatoes; cook for 10 minutes in covered pot. Add 3 quarts boiling water; cook 15 minutes more. Add string beans, peas, ditalini, salt and pepper; cover; cook slowly another 20 minutes.

Serve very hot. Sprinkle with parsley and cheese. Serves 6 to 8.

## MINESTRA DI PASTA E FAGIOLI

### PASTA AND KIDNEY BEAN SOUP

1 lb. kidney beans
½ cup chopped celery
1 large onion, minced
1 clove garlic
6 tbs. olive oil

1 chopped carrot
1 No. 2 can tomatoes
½ lb. tubettina (pasta)
½ cup grated Romano cheese
Salt and pepper to taste

† Ditalini: pasta; very short tubular type.

Soak beans overnight. Drain.

Cook beans in 3 quarts of salted boiling water in covered pot for 1 hour. Add all other ingredients except tubettini and olive oil. Cook slowly for 1 hour.

Cook tubettini in 3 quarts of rapidly boiling salted water about 10 minutes. Drain; add to beans and vegetables. Add olive oil; simmer about 15 minutes.

Serve very hot. Sprinkle with grated Romano cheese. Serves 6.

## MINESTRA DI ZIA TERESA

### AUNT TESSIE'S MINESTRA

| | |
|---|---|
| 1 lb. kidney beans | 4 qts. water |
| 3 bunches celery | 1 large onion, sliced |
| 1 clove garlic, chopped | 4 tbs. grated Romano |
| 1 tsp. orégano | cheese |
| 4 tbs. olive oil | Salt and pepper to taste |

Scrub and dice celery. Wash beans.

Place beans, celery, garlic, and onion in cold water; bring to a boil. Cover; simmer over very low flame about 1½ hours or until beans and celery are soft. Add oil, orégano, salt and pepper to taste. Simmer 15 minutes.

Serve very hot. Serves 4 to 6.

CHAPTER SIX

# Spaghetti and Pasta

## CAPPELLETTI

### LITTLE HATS

*Stuffing:*

1 lb. ricotta (Italian
  cottage cheese)
1 chicken breast
2 tbs. butter

1 whole egg
1 egg yolk
Pinch of nutmeg
Pinch of salt and pepper

3 tbs. grated Parmesan cheese

*Stuffing:* Brown chicken breast in butter; add salt and pepper to taste; chop very fine. Add it to other stuffing ingredients; mix thoroughly.

*Pasta:* (Dough)

1 lb. flour
3 eggs

1 cup lukewarm water
Pinch of salt

1 tbs. butter

*Pasta:* Place flour on board; beat eggs slightly; stir eggs into flour; add butter; gradually add enough water to form firm dough. Knead well until smooth and manageable. Cut in half; roll with rolling pin into thin sheets on lightly floured board. Cut into disks with a biscuit cutter; place 1 teaspoon stuffing on center of each disk; fold one side over to form the little hat. Press edges gently but firmly to prevent filling from falling out.

When all ingredients are used, drop the cappelletti into 6 quarts of rapidly boiling salted water; cook about 5 minutes or until dough is tender. Drain; put on hot platter; serve with plain tomato sauce and grated Parmesan cheese.

Cappelletti may also be boiled in chicken broth and served as soup.

## CONCHIGLIE E PATATE

### SEA SHELLS AND POTATOES

3/4 lb. conchiglie (pasta)
1½ lbs. potatoes
2 sliced onions
1 No. 2 can tomatoes

4 tbs. olive oil
2 tbs. chopped parsley
½ cup grated Pecorino
  cheese
Salt and pepper to taste

Peel and dice potatoes. Heat oil in large saucepan; add potatoes and onions. Cook 10 minutes; stir constantly to prevent burning. Add tomatoes, salt, pepper, and parsley; cover; cook over low flame for 30 minutes.

Cook conchiglie in 3 quarts of rapidly boiling salted water 20 minutes or until tender. Drain; place in large hot bowl; add hot sauce, potatoes, and cheese. Mix thoroughly.

Serve very hot. Serves 4 to 6.

## FUSILLI CON CAVOLFIORE

### FUSILLI WITH CAULIFLOWER

1 lb. fusilli (pasta)
1 small cauliflower
1 large diced onion
1 No. 2 can tomatoes
4 tbs. olive oil

1 tbs. pignoli (pine
  nuts)
1 tbs. currants
3 filets of anchovy
Salt and pepper to taste

Wash and break or cut cauliflower into small pieces. Cook in rapidly boiling salted water about 12 minutes or until tender but not soft. Drain; set aside.

Heat oil in saucepan; add onion; cook 3 minutes or until soft. Cut up anchovies; add; stir about 2 minutes or until dissolved. Add tomatoes; cover; simmer 20 minutes. Add cauliflower, pine nuts, currants, and very little salt and pepper. Mix well; keep hot over very low flame.

Cook fusilli in 4 quarts of rapidly boiling salted water 15 minutes or until tender. Drain; place in hot bowl; add cauliflower and sauce.

Serve very hot in individual plates. Serves 4 to 6. (If desired, Fusilli with Cauliflower may be sprinkled with grated Romano cheese just before serving.)

## GNOCCHI

### DUMPLINGS

4 lbs. potatoes                    5 cups flour
                   Salt to taste

Boil and rice potatoes. Gradually add 5 cups of flour. Knead until a smooth manageable dough is obtained. If necessary, add a little more flour.

Roll dough into long ropelike strips about ¾ inch thick; cut into ¾-inch pieces; dip in flour. Use prong of fork to make dented design on each piece.

Boil in 8 quarts of rapidly boiling salted water for about 10 minutes. Drain. Place on large platter or individual plates.

Serve with tomato sauce and sprinkle with grated Parmesan cheese. Serves 6 to 8.

## LASAGNE IMBOTTITE

### STUFFED NOODLES

*Sauce:*

1 large can plum to-         4 tbs. olive oil
    matoes                    2 cloves garlic
½ can tomato paste           1 stalk celery, diced
½ cup hot water              Salt and pepper to taste

*Stuffing:*

1½ lbs. ricotta (Italian     1½ cups cubed Mozza-
    cottage cheese)              rella
¾ lb. sausage               1½ cups grated Parmesan
1½ lbs. broad noodles           cheese
              Salt and pepper to taste

Blend tomato paste with hot water. Brown garlic in hot olive oil about 3 minutes; add celery, blended tomato paste and plum tomatoes; boil over high flame for 3 minutes; lower flame; cover; simmer for one hour. Add pepper and salt.

Broil sausage under high flame about 15 minutes or until brown on both sides; cut into small pieces.

Cook noodles in rapidly boiling salted water about 15 minutes or until tender, but not too soft. Drain.

Pour ½ cup sauce into bottom of baking pan; over this place layer of noodles, than layer of grated Parmesan cheese, a layer of sauce, a layer of Mozzarella, sausage, and a tablespoon of ricotta here and there. Repeat this process in layers until all ingredients are used. Top layer should be sauce and grated cheese. Bake in moderate oven for 15 minutes or until firm. When done, the Lasagne Imbottite is cut into serving portions. Place on individual plates; top with more sauce and grated cheese.

Serve very hot. Serves 8 to 10.

## LASAGNE AL FORNO

### BAKED NOODLES

*1 lb. noodles (½ in. wide)*
*1 small Mozzarella (¾ lb.)*
*½ cup grated Parmesan cheese*

*4 tbs. olive oil*
*1 large chopped onion*
*1 large can tomato purée*
*½ tsp. sugar*
*Salt and pepper to taste*

Brown onion in oil; add tomatoes, salt, pepper, and sugar. Cook slowly in covered pan for one hour; stir frequently.

Cook noodles about 15 minutes or until tender (stirring constantly to prevent sticking) in 5 quarts of rapidly boiling salted water. Drain. Alternate in baking dish layers of noodles, sauce, thin slices of Mozzarella, and a sprinkling of grated Parmesan cheese. Continue this process until all ingredients are used. Bake in moderate oven 15 minutes.

Serve very hot in individual dishes; top with more sauce and grated Parmesan cheese. Serves 4 to 6.

# MANICOTTI

## MACARONI MUFFS

*Pasta:* (Dough)

| | |
|---|---|
| *1 lb. flour* | *½ tsp. salt* |
| *1 cup lukewarm water* | *3 eggs* |
| | *1 tbs. butter* |

*Stuffing:*

| | |
|---|---|
| *1 lb. ricotta (Italian* | *2 eggs* |
| *cottage cheese)* | *½ cup grated Romano* |
| *¼ lb. chopped ham* | *cheese* |
| | *Salt and pepper to taste* |

Prepare plain Tomato Sauce #1.

*Pasta:* Mix flour, butter, 3 eggs, and salt. Gradually add enough water to make a medium-soft dough. Knead into a smooth ball. Cut into two sections and roll on lightly floured board until thin (the usual noodle thinness). Cut into rectangles, 5 by 6 inches.

*Stuffing:* Mix ricotta and eggs; add chopped ham. Use very little salt and pepper; keep mixing until well blended.

Spread 1½ tablespoons of mixture on each piece of dough; roll and close; moisten edges and press tightly to prevent filling from falling out. These are the little manicotti.

Cook manicotti about 10 minutes in extra-large pot of boiling salted water (about 8 quarts). When dough is tender, drain carefully with flat skimmer.

Place several manicotti on individual plates; cover manicotti with tomato sauce and a layer of grated Romano cheese.

Serve very hot. Serves 6 to 8.

# PASTA CON RICOTTA

## MACARONI WITH RICOTTA

*1 lb. any type cut maca-
    roni*
*1 lb. ricotta (Italian
    cottage cheese)*

*½ cup milk*
*2 ozs. butter*
*½ cup Parmesan cheese
    (grated)*

*Salt to taste*

Cook macaroni about 15 minutes or until tender in 5 quarts of rapidly boiling salted water. Drain; put back in pot; add butter.

Mix ricotta with milk in a bowl until smooth. Pour over hot macaroni; simmer 3 minutes over low flame in covered pot. Sprinkle with grated Parmesan cheese.

Serve very hot. Serves 4 to 6.

# RAVIOLI

*Pasta:* (Dough)

*3 cups flour*
*2 eggs*

*2 tbs. butter*
*1 cup warm water*

*¼ tsp. salt*

*Filling:*

*1 cup minced cooked
    chicken*
*1 cup chopped cooked
    spinach*
*½ cup bread crumbs*

*⅓ cup grated Parmesan
    cheese*
*2 eggs*
*2 tsp. chopped parsley*
*½ clove garlic, chopped*

*Salt and pepper to taste*

*Pasta:* Sift flour and salt together. Place on a board; drop eggs in center; add butter; mix. Gradually add enough water to make a rather stiff dough. Knead until smooth; cover and let stand about 10 minutes. Cut in half; roll on lightly floured board until very thin.

*Filling:* Beat eggs lightly. Blend all other ingredients; gradually add enough beaten egg to hold firmly together. Drop teaspoonfuls of filling about 2 inches apart on one sheet of dough until filling is used. Then cover with other sheet. With finger tips gently press around each mound of filling to form a little filled square. Cut squares apart with pastry cutter. Place 8 quarts of salted water in deep pot. When rapidly boiling, cook ravioli about 10 minutes or until dough is tender. Remove carefully with perforated soup skimmer; place serving portions on individual heated plates; top with Plain Tomato Sauce; sprinkle with grated Parmesan cheese.

Serve very hot. Serves 6.

## RIGATONI CON SALSICCIA

### RIGATONI WITH SAUSAGE

*1 lb. rigatoni (pasta)*
*1 lb. Italian pork sausage*
*3 tbs. olive oil*
*1 chopped onion*
*1 lb. fresh mushrooms*
*1 bay leaf*
*1 large can tomato purée*
*½ cup grated Pecorino cheese*
*1 clove garlic*
*Salt and pepper to taste*

Cut sausage in 1-inch pieces; place in hot skillet with olive oil; brown slightly for about 10 minutes. Add onion, mushrooms (well cleaned and sliced), garlic, salt, and pepper; simmer for 15 minutes. Add tomato purée and bay leaf. Cover pan; cook slowly for 1 hour. Remove bay leaf.

Cook rigatoni about 20 minutes in 5 quarts of rapidly boiling salted water. When tender, drain and place in baking dish. Add sausage and sauce. Mix. Sprinkle with grated Pecorino cheese. Bake in moderate oven about 10 minutes.

Serve very hot. Serves 6.

## SPAGHETTI CON ACCIUGHE

### SPAGHETTI WITH ANCHOVIES

*1 lb. spaghetti*
*½ cup olive oil*
*1 clove garlic*
*12 filets of anchovy*
*½ cup grated Parmesan cheese*
*Salt and pepper to taste*

Fry garlic in hot oil about 3 minutes or until brown. Then remove garlic. Cut anchovies in ½-inch pieces and add to hot oil; cook for 2 minutes; stir constantly. Add a little pepper.

Cook spaghetti about 20 minutes or until tender in rapidly boiling salted water. Drain; arrange on individual heated plates. Pour sauce over spaghetti. Top with grated Parmesan cheese. Use salt very sparingly since anchovies are very salty. Serves 4 to 6.

## SPAGHETTI AL BURRO

### SPAGHETTI WITH BUTTER

*1 lb. spaghetti*  
*¼ lb. butter*  

*2 ozs. grated Parmesan*  
*cheese*  
*Salt to taste*

Cook spaghetti in 5 quarts of rapidly boiling salted water for 20 minutes. Drain. Melt butter in saucepan over low flame. Serve spaghetti in heated individual plates. Pour melted butter over steaming spaghetti; sprinkle with grated Parmesan cheese.

Serve immediately. Serves 4 to 6.

## SPAGHETTI E FINOCCHIO SICILIANA

### SPAGHETTI WITH FENNEL SICILIAN

*1 lb. spaghetti*  
*1 lb. thin fresh finocchio*  
*4 tbs. olive oil*  
*1 chopped onion*  
*1 cup cold water*  

*1 lb. fresh sardines*  
*1½ cups toasted bread*  
*crumbs*  
*1 tbs. pine nuts*  
*1 tbs. seedless raisins*  
*Salt and pepper to taste*

Clean and bone sardines.

Clean finocchio. Cook in 1 quart of boiling salted water

about 15 minutes or until tender. Drain; cut into half-inch pieces.

Cook onion in olive oil, in saucepan, about 3 minutes or until golden brown; add sardines; sauté 10 minutes, stirring frequently to prevent burning; add finocchio, raisins, and pine nuts; add cup of cold water, salt and pepper; simmer slowly for about 10 minutes. The fish may break up during this process.

Cook spaghetti about 20 minutes in 5 quarts of rapidly boiling salted water. Drain; put in deep dish; add half of finocchio mixture to the spaghetti; sprinkle with half of toasted bread crumbs. Mix. Serve on individual plates. Top with bread crumbs and more finocchio mixture. No cheese is used.

Serve very hot. Serves 6. This is a traditional St. Joseph's Day dish.

## SPAGHETTI CON SALSA DI CARNE

### SPAGHETTI WITH MEAT SAUCE

| | |
|---|---|
| *1 lb. spaghetti* | *1 large can plum toma-* |
| *½ clove garlic* | *toes* |
| *½ lb. chopped beef* | *½ cup grated Pecorino* |
| *1 chopped onion* | *cheese* |
| *2 tsp. chopped parsley* | *4 tbs. olive oil* |

*½ cup chopped mushrooms*
*Salt and pepper to taste*

Fry chopped beef in hot oil about 10 minutes or until slightly brown. Add garlic, onion, mushrooms, and parsley; sauté for 10 minutes. Stir occasionally. Add salt, pepper, and tomatoes; simmer 1 hour or until sauce is of thick consistency.

Cook spaghetti 20 minutes in 5 quarts of rapidly boiling salted water. Drain. Place on heated serving dish; add hot sauce; sprinkle with grated Pecorino cheese. Any type macaroni may be served with this meat sauce.

Serves 4 to 6.

## SPAGHETTI MARINARA

### SPAGHETTI WITH MARINER SAUCE

1 lb. spaghetti
1 large can plum toma-
   toes
4 tbs. olive oil
2 sliced onions
1 clove garlic

2 ozs. grated Romano
   cheese
¼ tsp. orégano
¼ tsp. sugar
2 filets of anchovy
Salt and pepper to taste

Sauté onion and garlic in hot oil about 5 minutes or until soft; remove garlic; add tomatoes; cook rapidly for 5 minutes; then lower flame and simmer for 1 hour. Add anchovies cut into small pieces. Use very little salt and pepper; add sugar. Cook slowly for 10 minutes. Add orégano; stir. Keep hot over low flame until ready to serve.

Cook spaghetti as usual. Drain; arrange on hot platter and pour sauce over spaghetti. Sprinkle with grated cheese.

Serves 4 to 6.

## SPAGHETTI CON MELENZANI

### SPAGHETTI WITH EGGPLANT

1 lb. spaghetti
1 large eggplant
1 large can plum to-
   matoes
1 clove garlic
1 tbs. chopped parsley

1 minced onion
2 ozs. grated Parmesan
   cheese
4 tbs. olive oil
½ cup peanut oil
Salt and pepper to taste

Place olive oil in saucepan; add onion, garlic, and parsley; cook 3 minutes. Add tomatoes, salt and pepper; simmer slowly for 1 hour. Stir frequently.

Meanwhile, peel eggplant; slice it lengthwise about ½ inch thick; sprinkle a little salt on each slice; put in colander and allow to drain for 15 minutes. Then rinse in cold water; pat dry with absorbent paper. Fry slices in hot peanut oil about 3 minutes on each side or until light brown and soft. When done, set eggplant aside and keep hot.

Cook spaghetti as usual. Drain; place on hot platter and

pour tomato sauce over spaghetti. Cut eggplant slices in half or in thin strips; arrange over tomato sauce and sprinkle generously with grated Parmesan cheese.

Serve hot. Serves 4 to 6.

## SPAGHETTI CON SALSÀ SEMPLICE DI POMODORO

### SPAGHETTI WITH PLAIN TOMATO SAUCE

*1 large can tomato purée*　　*1 lb. spaghetti*
*2 cloves garlic*　　　　　　*2 ozs. grated Romano*
*4 tbs. olive oil*　　　　　　　*cheese*
*1 bay leaf*　　　　　　　　*½ tsp. sugar*
*Salt and pepper to taste*

Heat olive oil in saucepan; add garlic and brown for 2 minutes; add tomato purée, sugar, bay leaf, salt and pepper. Cook over low flame for 1 hour. Stir frequently to prevent burning. Then remove bay leaf and garlic.

Cook spaghetti about 20 minutes or until tender, in rapidly boiling salted water. Drain; place on heated platter.

Pour sauce over spaghetti; sprinkle generously with grated Romano cheese.

Serve very hot. Serves 4 to 6.

## SPAGHETTI CON SALSA DI VONGOLI

### SPAGHETTI WITH CLAM SAUCE

### See recipe for Clam Sauce

Boil one pound of spaghetti or other type macaroni for about 15 minutes in 5 quarts of rapidly boiling salted water. It will be *al dente,* which means medium. Or cook until soft, if you prefer it that way.

Drain; arrange on heated platter or individual serving dishes and pour very hot Clam Sauce over it.

This appetizing dish may be served with or without grated Romano cheese.

Serves 4 to 6.

## SPAGHETTINI BAGARIA

### THIN SPAGHETTI BAGARIA STYLE

1 lb. spaghettini
4 tbs. olive oil
2 cloves garlic
1 large can plum toma-
  toes
1 small eggplant, diced
1 tbs. capers (washed)

2 leaves sweet basil,
  chopped
½ cup grated Pecorino
  cheese
2 tbs. chopped green
  olives
Salt and pepper to taste

Heat olive oil in saucepan; brown garlic 2 minutes; then add tomatoes, salt and pepper to taste. Stir. Add olives, capers, and basil. Cover pan and simmer over very low flame 45 minutes. Add diced eggplant; simmer 20 minutes longer or until eggplant is tender.

Cook spaghettini 12 minutes in 4 quarts of rapidly boiling salted water. When tender, drain; arrange on hot platter. Pour hot sauce over this; sprinkle with grated Pecorino cheese.

Serve very hot. Serves 4 to 6.

## TAGLIARINI CON FEGATINI

### NARROW NOODLES WITH CHICKEN LIVERS

¾ lb. tagliarini (narrow
  noodles)
¾ lb. chicken livers
4 tbs. olive oil
½ cup grated Incane-
  strato cheese

1 large can tomatoes
1 cup cooked or canned
  peas
1 clove garlic, chopped
Salt and pepper to taste

Chop livers; brown in hot oil. Add garlic, salt, pepper, and tomatoes. Cover; simmer slowly for 40 minutes. Add peas; simmer for 20 minutes longer.

Cook noodles in rapidly boiling salted water, as usual. When tender, drain; arrange on heated platter and pour hot sauce over them. Sprinkle with grated Incanestrato cheese.

Serve very hot. Serves 4.

## TAGLIARINI CON SPARAGI
### NARROW EGG NOODLES WITH ASPARAGUS

*1 lb. narrow egg noodles*
*2 lbs. fresh asparagus*
*4 tbs. olive oil*
*1 large can plum*
*   tomatoes*

*½ cup grated Parmesan*
*   cheese*
*2 small cloves garlic*
*Salt and pepper to taste*

Clean asparagus and remove tough stalks. Cut in half. Dry them.

Heat olive oil in large saucepan. Add garlic and asparagus; sauté 10 minutes over low flame. Add tomatoes, salt and pepper to taste; cover; simmer slowly 1 hour. Stir occasionally to prevent burning.

Cook noodles about 12 minutes or until tender in 5 quarts of rapidly boiling salted water. Drain; place on hot platter; cover with sauce and asparagus. Sprinkle generously with grated Parmesan cheese.

Serve very hot. Serves 4 to 6.


## TORTA DI DITALI
### DITALI PIE

*¾ lb. cooked ditali*
*   (pasta)*
*1½ cups Plain Tomato*
*   Sauce*
*½ cup grated Romano*
*   cheese*

*1 cup cooked chopped*
*   meat*
*2 eggs*
*Salt and pepper to taste*

Make a rich flaky pastry as for pie. Line a 10-inch deep-dish pie plate or casserole.

Mix cooked ditali, tomato sauce, cheese, and meat; place over pastry. Beat eggs thoroughly; pour evenly over all. Cover with pastry; bake in moderate oven about 25 minutes or until pastry is golden brown.

Cut in individual portions and serve hot, with mixed salad. Serves 6.

# CHAPTER SEVEN

# Sauces

## SALSA CON ACCIUGHE

### ANCHOVY SAUCE

10 anchovies (filets)
2 tbs. vinegar
1 clove garlic

2 tbs. olive oil
4 hard-boiled egg yolks
½ cup chopped parsley

Put anchovies, garlic, and oil in pan; cook slowly about 5 minutes or until anchovies are dissolved. Gradually add parsley, vinegar, mashed egg yolks; stir constantly to blend well. If too thick, add a tablespoon of hot water and a tablespoon of vinegar. Stir. Remove from fire. Cool.

Serve cold on cold meats or fish.

## SALSA DI CAPPERI

### CAPER SAUCE

1 oz. capers
2 ozs. butter
1 tsp. flour

2 tbs. vinegar
1 tsp. chopped parsley
½ cup meat broth

Salt and pepper to taste

Wash and chop capers. Place butter in saucepan; heat over low flame. Gradually add flour, stirring constantly until smooth, light brown. Add capers, vinegar, parsley, salt and pepper to taste; stir constantly. Add broth. Simmer for 10 minutes. Serve hot over boiled or baked fish.

## SALSA CON CARNE

### MEAT SAUCE

*1 can tomato paste*            *1 chopped onion*
*2 tbs. olive oil*              *1 bay leaf*
*1 clove garlic*               *½ lb. chopped lean beef*
*2½ cups warm water*              *or pork*
                   *Salt and pepper to taste*

Brown onion, garlic, and meat in olive oil in saucepan for about 10 minutes. Add paste; stir; cook 3 minutes longer. Add salt and pepper, water, bay leaf. Cover; simmer for 1 hour. Remove bay leaf; simmer 30 minutes longer.

## SALSO CON CARNE E FUNGHI

### MEAT AND MUSHROOM SAUCE

*½ lb. chopped beef*            *1 cup boiled sliced*
*¼ cup olive oil*                *mushrooms*
*½ can tomato paste*            *1 clove garlic*
*⅛ tsp. crushed red*            *1 large can plum*
*pepper seeds*                  *tomatoes*
                   *Salt to taste*

Heat oil in saucepan; add mushrooms, garlic, pepper seeds, beef; simmer 5 minutes; stir frequently. Add tomatoes; simmer over low flame for 45 minutes. Stir occasionally; add tomato paste and blend; stir; add salt. Cover. Simmer for 30 minutes more; stir occasionally to prevent sticking. The longer this cooks, the better the flavor. Keep hot over very low flame until ready to use. This is enough sauce for 1½ pounds of spaghetti or any type macaroni. Serves 6 to 8.

## SALSA DI FUNGHI E POMODORO

### MUSHROOM AND TOMATO SAUCE

| | |
|---|---|
| *1 lb. mushrooms* | *2 sweet basil leaves* |
| *1 large can plum* | *1 large clove garlic* |
| *tomatoes* | *Pinch of crushed red* |
| *4 tbs. olive oil* | *pepper seeds* |
| *Salt to taste* | |

Wash and slice mushrooms. Place olive oil in saucepan; brown garlic 2 minutes. Add mushrooms; simmer for 10 minutes. Mash tomatoes and add; stir; add pepper seeds, basil leaves, and salt. Cover. Simmer for 1 hour over low flame. Stir occasionally to prevent sticking. Pour over spaghetti when steaming hot. Enough sauce for 1½ pounds of any type pasta. Sprinkle with Pecorino cheese if desired.

## SALSA PICCANTE

### PIQUANT SAUCE

| | |
|---|---|
| *1 cup burgundy or dry* | *2 cloves garlic, chopped* |
| *sauterne* | *¼ cup wine vinegar* |
| *1 cup olive oil* | *⅛ tsp. dried red pepper* |
| *2 chopped onions* | *seeds* |
| *Pinch of rosemary* | *¼ tsp. salt* |

Mix all ingredients thoroughly. Stir constantly until well blended. Put in jar to marinate for 24 hours. Remove garlic. Good with cold meats and fowl. Also may be used to baste meats and fowl while roasting or broiling. Imparts exotic flavor.

## SALSA DI PISELLI

### PEA SAUCE

| | |
|---|---|
| *3 tbs. olive oil* | *2 cups fresh peas,* |
| *1 sliced onion* | *shelled* |
| *1 strip bacon, chopped* | *1 cup water* |
| *1 tsp. chopped parsley* | *Salt and pepper to taste* |

Cook onion in olive oil about 5 minutes or until soft. Add chopped bacon; simmer 3 minutes. Add parsley; stir. Add water and peas, salt and pepper; cook slowly for 20 minutes or until peas are done.

This sauce may be used on any type macaroni or rice. Grated Parmesan cheese may also be sprinkled over top for added flavor.

## SALSA SEMPLICE DI POMODORO #1

### PLAIN TOMATO SAUCE #1

1 large can tomatoes  ½ tsp. sugar
4 tbs. olive oil   1 clove garlic
2 sliced onions   1 sprig sweet basil
   Salt and pepper to taste

Fry sliced onion and garlic in oil about 5 minutes; add basil. Strain tomatoes through sieve; add and simmer for 45 minutes or until tomatoes are cooked to a thick sauce. Stir frequently. Add sugar, salt, and pepper; stir thoroughly. Simmer 15 minutes.

This sauce may be used on any type macaroni or boiled rice. Sufficient for 1 pound. Also used with Pizza recipe.

## SALSA SEMPLICE DI POMODORO #2

### PLAIN TOMATO SAUCE #2

1 can tomato paste  ½ tsp. orégano
3 tbs. olive oil   2½ cups water
2 large onions, sliced  Salt and pepper to taste

Fry onion in oil about 5 minutes or until medium brown. Add paste; fry 3 minutes, stirring constantly. Add orégano, salt and pepper to taste; also 2½ cups water; cover. Simmer over low flame for 25 minutes.

Easily and quickly prepared. May be used on any type macaroni. Sufficient for 1 pound. Serve very hot.

# SALSA TARTUFATA

### TRUFFLE SAUCE

½ cup sliced truffles          1 tsp. flour
¾ cup bouillon or broth        1 tsp. chopped parsley
¼ cup dry sherry               1 sliced onion
2 tbs. butter                  1 small clove garlic
                 Salt and pepper to taste

Place butter in saucepan and melt over low flame. Brown garlic, onion, and parsley lightly for about 2 minutes. Blend flour with sherry and add; lower flame; stir constantly until very smooth. Add truffles, bouillon, salt and pepper to taste; cover; simmer for about 20 minutes. Excellent over roasts and veal cutlets. Serve hot.

# SALSA DI VONGOLI

### CLAM SAUCE

1 doz. little-neck clams       4 tbs. olive oil
2 cloves garlic                1 large can tomatoes
1 tbs. chopped parsley         Salt and pepper to taste

Scrub clams; rinse in cold running water until all sand is removed. Insert thin knife blade between edges of shells and pry open. Cut clams into small pieces. Place clams with juice in bowl.

Brown garlic in hot oil in saucepan; add clam juice, strained tomatoes, chopped parsley, salt and pepper to taste. Simmer slowly for 40 minutes; add clams; turn up flame; cook for only 2 minutes. Prolonged cooking toughens clams.

Enough for 4 to 6 portions. Sufficient sauce for 1 pound of spaghetti or other macaroni. Grated cheese is not generally used with this sauce.

# CHAPTER EIGHT

# Sea Foods

## Fish

### BACCALÀ DOLCE E AGRO
#### DRY COD SWEET AND SOUR

*1 whole dry cod (about
  2 lbs.)
2 tbs. currants or seed-
  less raisins
1 tbs. shelled pistachio
  nuts*

*½ cup olive or peanut oil
1 clove garlic
½ cup flour
½ cup vinegar
⅔ cup water
1 tbs. chopped fresh mint*

*Pinch of pepper*

Soak cod in cold water 24 hours. Change water several times. Wash in cold water before using. Dry with absorbent paper; cut in serving pieces. Roll in flour.

Heat oil in skillet; brown garlic 3 minutes; remove from oil. Fry cod in hot oil about 5 minutes on each side or until light brown and tender.

In separate saucepan blend vinegar, water, currants, mint, and pistachio nuts; boil slowly 5 minutes. Pour hot sauce over cod; cover; simmer slowly 3 minutes.

Serve very hot with green salad. Serves 4.

### BACCALÀ FIORENTINA
#### DRY COD FLORENTINE

*1 whole dry cod (about
  2 lbs.)
2 cloves garlic
3 tbs. tomato paste
2 sprigs fresh mint*

*1 tsp. washed capers
½ cup olive or peanut oil
½ cup flour
1 cup warm water
Pinch of pepper to taste*

Soak fish in cold water 24 hours. Change water several times. Wash in cold water before cooking.

Cut fish in 4-inch serving pieces. Roll in flour.

Heat oil in skillet; brown garlic 3 minutes; fry cod 3 or 4 minutes on each side until light brown. Sprinkle lightly with pepper to taste.

Blend tomato paste with warm water; pour over fish; add mint and capers; cover; simmer about 10 minutes or until tender and well done.

Serve very hot. Serves 4.

## CALAMAI CON POMODORO

### SQUIDS WITH TOMATOES

| | |
|---|---|
| 2 lbs. squids | 1 cup solid-pack toma- |
| 4 tbs. olive oil | toes |
| Pinch of orégano | ½ cup dry sherry |
| 1 tsp. chopped parsley | 2 cloves garlic |

Salt and pepper to taste

Have squids thoroughly cleaned. Cut into small pieces. Wash well.

Pour olive oil in saucepan and heat; brown garlic about 3 minutes. Add squids; cover; sauté 10 minutes. Add salt, pepper, orégano, and sherry; cook 10 minutes longer over low flame. Add tomatoes, parsley; cover; cook 15 minutes or until tender.

Serve very hot on toast. Serves 4 to 6.

## CAPITONE FRITTO

### FRIED EELS

| | |
|---|---|
| 2½ lbs. thick eels | 1 cup flour |
| 6 tbs. olive oil | 1 tsp. rosemary |

Salt and pepper to taste

Have eels skinned and cleaned. Cut crosswise in 3-inch pieces. Dry; roll in flour; add salt and pepper. Sprinkle with rosemary. Fry over medium flame about 10 minutes or until golden brown on both sides.

Serve hot with lemon slices. Serves 4 to 6.

This is a Christmas Eve specialty.

## ANGUILLE MARINATE

### MARINATED EELS

Follow same procedure as for fried eels (Capitone Fritto). Put fried eels in deep dish. Then prepare this dressing:

| | |
|---|---|
| *¾ cup wine vinegar* | *1 large onion, sliced* |
| *¾ cup water* | *1 bay leaf* |
| *1 clove garlic* | *Pinch of rosemary* |
| | *Salt and pepper to taste* |

Strain and use leftover oil after frying eels.

Combine vinegar and water; boil for 2 minutes; sauté garlic and onion in hot oil about 5 minutes or until medium soft. Add vinegar, water, bay leaf, rosemary, salt and pepper to taste; cook 5 minutes over low flame. Remove; cool. Pour prepared liquid over eels. Set aside in refrigerator.

May be served cold at any time. Marinating the eels several hours improves the flavor.

## MERLUZZO LESSO

### BOILED WHITING

| | |
|---|---|
| *2 lbs. whiting* | *3 tbs. olive oil* |
| *1 clove garlic, chopped* | *1½ cups warm water* |
| *2 tbs. chopped parsley* | *Salt and pepper to taste* |

Have fish cleaned. Wash thoroughly. Cut in half crosswise. Place olive oil, parsley, and garlic in saucepan; cook about 3 minutes or until garlic is soft. Add warm water and allow to come to a boil. Add fish, salt, and pepper;

cover; simmer 10 minutes over low flame. Serve in own broth.

Serve very hot. Serves 4.

## MERLUZZO CON SALSA DI POMODORO

### WHITING WITH TOMATO SAUCE

2 lbs. whiting
1 clove garlic, chopped
2 tbs. chopped parsley
1 No. 2 can tomatoes
1 minced onion
1 diced carrot
4 tbs. olive oil
Salt and pepper to taste

Have fish cleaned. Wash thoroughly. Cut crosswise, in half. Brown onion and garlic in oil; add carrot and parsley; cook slowly 5 minutes. Add tomatoes, salt, and pepper; cover; cook over slow flame 25 minutes longer. Add fish; cover; continue cooking slowly 10 minutes or until fish is tender.

Serve very hot with sauce. Serves 4.

## FRITELLE DI PESCIOLINI

### MINNOW PANCAKES

1 lb. minnows
2 eggs
1 clove garlic, chopped
1 tbs. chopped parsley
½ cup peanut oil
3 tbs. grated Romano
cheese
1 cup flour
¼ cup bread crumbs
1 tsp. chopped sweet basil
Salt and pepper to taste

Wash and clean minnows. Drain. Place in deep mixing bowl. Add eggs, salt, pepper, cheese, basil, parsley, bread crumbs, and garlic. Add enough flour for easy molding. Form into small pancakes, about 3 inches in diameter. Roll in flour.

Pour oil in skillet and heat; fry pancakes quickly, about 5 minutes or until golden brown.

Serve very hot. Serves 4.

## SALMONE LESSO

### BOILED SALMON

| | |
|---|---|
| 2 lbs. salmon | 1 sliced onion |
| 3 cups water | 2 cloves |
| 1 tbs. chopped parsley | 1 sliced lemon |
| 1 sliced carrot | ½ cup diced celery |
| 3 tbs. olive oil | Salt and pepper to taste |

Have salmon sliced about 2 inches thick.

Boil all ingredients except salmon and lemon about 20 minutes. Add salmon; cover; cook 15 minutes or until tender.

Serve very hot with own broth. Garnish with lemon slices. Serves 4.

## SARDE BECCAFICO

### STUFFED SARDINES

2 lbs. fresh sardines

Clean each sardine carefully. Slit down center to form an open filet and remove bones.

*Stuffing:*

| | |
|---|---|
| 1½ cups bread crumbs | ¼ cup grated Romano |
| 2 tbs. chopped parsley | cheese |
| 4 tbs. olive oil | 1 clove garlic, chopped |
| Salt and pepper to taste | |

Mix thoroughly all ingredients except olive oil; gradually add oil to make a firm mixture. If needed, add another teaspoon of oil.

Cover whole filet with stuffing; top with another filet to form a sandwich. Tie with white thread so stuffing does not fall out. Continue this until all are used.

*Sauce:*

| | |
|---|---|
| *3 tbs. olive oil* | *1 clove garlic, chopped* |
| *1 tbs. chopped sweet basil or parsley* | *1 No. 2 can tomato purée* |

*Salt and pepper to taste*

Pour olive oil in large shallow pan; add garlic, parsley or basil; cook 3 minutes. Add tomato purée, salt and pepper to taste; simmer over slow fire 25 minutes. Stir frequently. Place fish very carefully in sauce; cover pan; cook over low flame 15 minutes or until fish is tender.

Prepare hot platter. Remove fish carefully and put on platter. Remove thread by cutting; pour sauce over fish.

Serve very hot. Serves 4 to 6.

## SGOMBRO RIPIENO

### STUFFED MACKEREL

| | |
|---|---|
| *3 mackerel (about 1 lb. each)* | *¼ cup fresh mushrooms, chopped* |
| *6 tbs. olive oil* | *1 tbs. chopped parsley* |
| *1 chopped onion* | *1 tsp. fresh mint, chopped* |
| *1 cup bread crumbs* | *1 sliced lemon* |
| *¼ cup grated Romano cheese* | *Salt and pepper to taste* |

Have fish cleaned, slit down center, and boned. Sprinkle inside with salt.

*Stuffing:* Heat half of olive oil in saucepan. Sauté onion, mushrooms, and parsley about 15 minutes or until mushrooms are tender. Set aside.

Mix in deep bowl the bread crumbs, mint, cheese, salt and pepper to taste. Add to mushroom mixture. Blend well. Stuff fish. Skewer or sew edges together; place stuffed fish with balance of oil in baking pan; bake in hot oven 15 minutes; reduce heat. Baste occasionally with pan oil and cook 15 minutes longer or until fish is tender.

Serve very hot with lemon slices. Serves 4 to 6.

## SPADA ALLA GRIGLIA

### BROILED SWORDFISH

| | |
|---|---|
| 2 lbs. swordfish | ¼ cup olive oil |
| Juice of 2 lemons | 2 tsp. orégano |
| 1 tsp. fresh mint, chopped | Salt and pepper to taste |

Have fish sliced 1½ inches thick. Wash. Dry.

Blend well oil, lemon juice, orégano, mint, salt, and pepper. Brush fish with this.

Place on preheated broiler rack about 4 inches below flame.

Broil 5 minutes or until slightly brown; turn; brush again with mixture. Broil about 7 minutes or until done. Brush again with mixture before serving.

Serve hot. Serves 4 to 6.

## FILETTI DI SOGLIOLE PIZZAIOLA

### FILET OF SOLE PIZZAIOLA*

| | |
|---|---|
| 1 lb. filet of sole | ½ cup bread crumbs |
| 1 tbs. orégano | ½ cup canned plum |
| 1 tbs. chopped parsley | tomatoes |
| Juice of 1 lemon | Salt and pepper to taste |

¼ cup olive oil or melted butter

Blend thoroughly bread crumbs, orégano, parsley, salt and pepper to taste. Roll fish in this mixture.

Put half of oil or butter in baking dish; place breaded filet in dish. Spread tomatoes over fish; pour balance of oil or melted butter over this.

Bake in hot oven 10 minutes or until tender. Serve steaming hot with lemon juice. Serves 4.

* Aunt Lena's recipe. *Pizzaiola* means "like a little pie."

## SPINOLA RIPIENA

### STUFFED STRIPED BASS

| | |
|---|---|
| *1 striped bass (about 4 lbs.)* | *Pinch of marjoram* |
| *5 tbs. olive oil* | *3 tbs. grated Romano cheese* |
| *2 cups bread crumbs* | *½ cup chopped celery* |
| *1 large onion, chopped* | *1 small clove garlic, chopped* |
| *Juice of 1 lemon* | |
| *1 tsp. thyme* | *Salt and pepper to taste* |

Have fish cleaned, slit down center, and boned. Sprinkle inside with salt.

*Stuffing:* Place 3 tablespoons olive oil in saucepan; add celery, onion, and garlic; cook about 10 minutes or until soft. Remove from fire.

Mix thoroughly in bowl bread crumbs, salt, pepper, thyme, cheese, marjoram; add this to celery, onion, and garlic. Blend well. Stuff fish. Skewer or sew edges together to prevent stuffing from falling out. Place in baking pan. Brush fish with remaining oil. Bake in hot oven 10 minutes. Then lower heat; bake in moderate oven about 20 minutes or until fish is tender. If pan gets too dry, add about ¼ cup hot water. Baste fish. Add lemon juice before serving.

Serve very hot. Serves 6.

## STOCCO SCIACCA

### STOCKFISH SCIACCA

| | |
|---|---|
| *2 lbs. soaked stockfish* | *½ cup olive oil* |
| *1 tsp. orégano* | *1 No. 2 can tomatoes* |
| *1 tbs. capers* | *10 ripe black olives* |
| *1 tbs. chopped sweet basil* | *1 clove garlic* |
| | *Salt and pepper to taste* |

Cut stockfish† into serving pieces about 3 inches long. Wash in cold running water; dry with absorbent paper.

† Stockfish, a species of dry cod, may be purchased in Italian fish markets. It is soaked and prepared for use as given in this recipe.

Fry in ¼ cup of oil 10 minutes or until golden brown on both sides. Remove from pan.

Meanwhile, cook garlic 2 minutes in balance of oil in saucepan; when light brown add tomatoes, salt, and pepper; cover; cook for 20 minutes over low flame. Add fish, olives, basil, capers, orégano; cook 15 minutes.

Serve very hot. Serves 6.

## STOCCO PALERMITANA

### STOCKFISH PALERMO

| | |
|---|---|
| *2 lbs. soaked stockfish* | *½ lb. diced potatoes* |
| *1 cup stewed or canned* | *½ cup olive oil* |
| *tomatoes* | *¼ lb. chopped green* |
| *1 tbs. washed capers* | *olives* |
| *1 sliced onion* | *½ cup diced celery* |

*Salt and pepper to taste*

Cut soaked stockfish into 3-inch pieces. Wash in cold running water.

Heat oil in large saucepan; sauté fish and all ingredients except tomatoes for 15 minutes. Stir frequently. Add tomatoes and enough warm water to cover all. Lower flame; add very little salt, pepper; cover; cook slowly about 10 minutes or until fish and potatoes are tender.

Serve hot. Serves 6.

## TONNO AGRO E DOLCE

### TUNA SOUR AND SWEET

| | |
|---|---|
| *2 lbs. fresh tuna fish* | *6 tbs. wine vinegar* |
| *½ cup peanut or olive oil* | *1½ tsp. sugar* |
| *2 large onions, sliced* | *Salt and pepper to taste* |

*4 sprigs fresh mint or sweet basil, chopped*

Have tuna fish sliced 1½ inches thick. Season with salt and pepper to taste. Pour oil in skillet; heat; fry fish about 10 minutes or until brown on both sides. Remove fish. Set aside.

Cook onion slowly in same oil about 5 minutes or until soft; add vinegar, mint or basil, and sugar. Cover; cook slowly 5 minutes more. Place fish in hot sauce; cover; cook slowly 3 minutes longer. Serve very hot.

Fish may also be served cold. If so, cool sauce; pour over fish; marinate several hours in cool place. The longer it marinates, the better the flavor.

Serves 4 to 6.

## TONNO ALLA GRIGLIA
### BROILED TUNA FISH

| | |
|---|---|
| 2 lbs. fresh tuna fish | 1 tbs. chopped parsley |
| 4 tbs. olive oil | 1 tsp. fresh mint, |
| ½ clove garlic chopped | chopped |
| 1½ cups bread crumbs | 1 lemon |
| | Salt and pepper to taste |

Have fish sliced 1½ inches thick. Wash; dry with damp cloth. Rub with a little oil; sprinkle lightly with salt and pepper.

Mix bread crumbs, garlic, parsley, and mint. Roll fish in this mixture. Pour a little oil over each slice. Place on preheated broiler rack, about 4 inches below medium flame; broil about 7 minutes on each side or until tender.

Serve very hot with lemon slices. Serves 4.

## TONNO CON SALSA DI POMODORO
### FRESH TUNA WITH TOMATO SAUCE

| | |
|---|---|
| 2 lbs. fresh tuna fish | 1 clove garlic |
| 4 tbs. olive oil | 1 small onion, sliced |
| 1 tbs. chopped parsley | ½ can tomato paste |
| 2 cups hot water | Salt and pepper to taste |

Have fish sliced 1½ inches thick. Wash; dry with absorbent paper; sprinkle with salt and pepper to taste.

Pour oil in skillet; add onion, garlic, parsley; cook 5 minutes or until soft.

Blend tomato paste in 2 cups of hot water; add to mixture in skillet; cover; simmer 20 minutes, stirring occasionally. Add fish; cover; cook 15 minutes or until tender. Serve very hot. Serves 4.

## TROTA CON ACCIUGHE

### TROUT WITH ANCHOVY

| | |
|---|---|
| 6 trout | 1 cup flour |
| 6 tbs. olive oil | 3 tbs. butter |
| 4 filets of anchovy | 1 tsp. fresh mint, |
| 1 cup dry sherry | chopped |
| Juice of 1 lemon | 1 tsp. chopped parsley |

Salt and pepper to taste

Clean trout; dry with absorbent paper; salt and pepper to taste; roll in flour. Fry slowly in hot olive oil about 10 minutes or until brown.

Melt butter in saucepan over low flame. Add anchovy filets cut into small pieces; cook about 5 minutes. Add sherry; cover; simmer 1 minute. Add mint and parsley; simmer 3 minutes. Add lemon juice.

Place fish on hot platter; pour sauce over it. Serve very hot. Serves 4 to 6.

## Shellfish

## ARAGOSTA FRA DIAVOLO

### LOBSTER FRA DIAVOLO

| | |
|---|---|
| 2 lobsters (about 1½ lbs. each) | ¼ cup olive oil |
| 2 tbs. chopped parsley | ¼ tsp. crushed red pepper seeds |
| 1 clove garlic, chopped | 1 tsp. orégano |
| 2 cups canned plum tomatoes | Salt and pepper to taste |

Insert sharp knife between body and tail of lobster to sever spinal cord. Place on back and split to end of tail. Spread open. The green and coral parts are edible, but be sure to remove the small sac just back of the head. Crack large claws.

Place lobster cut side up in large flat baking dish. Set aside.

Pour olive oil in saucepan; heat; brown garlic 2 minutes. Add tomatoes, parsley, orégano, pepper seeds, salt, and very little pepper. Simmer 10 minutes. Pour sauce evenly over top of lobster. Bake in moderately hot oven about 20 minutes or until lobster meat is tender.

Serve very hot. Serves 4.

## ARAGOSTA ALLA MARSALA

### LOBSTER MARSALA

| | |
|---|---|
| *1 large lobster (1½ lbs.)* | *4 tbs. olive oil* |
| *1 tbs. chopped parsley* | *2 cloves garlic* |
| *½ cup marsala* | *Salt and pepper to taste* |

Insert sharp knife between body and tail of lobster to sever spinal cord. Do not remove from shell. Clean; cut into small serving pieces; crack claws.

Pour oil in saucepan; brown garlic about 3 minutes; remove from oil. Add lobster, salt and pepper, parsley. Cover; simmer over low flame for 20 minutes or until tender. Add marsala; simmer 2 minutes.

Serve very hot. Serves 2.

## ARAGOSTA OREGANATA

### LOBSTER ORÉGANO

| | |
|---|---|
| *1 large lobster (about 2 lbs.)* | *1 tbs. chopped parsley* |
| *6 tbs. olive oil* | *2 tbs. grated Parmesan. cheese* |
| *1 clove garlic, chopped* | *½ tsp. orégano* |
| *1 tsp. chopped sweet basil* | *½ cup bread crumbs* |
| | *Salt and pepper to taste* |

Insert sharp knife between body and tail of lobster to sever spinal cord. Place on back and split to end of tail. Spread open. The green and coral parts are edible, but be sure to remove the small sac just back of the head. Crack large claws.

Place in baking pan, cut side up; add ½ cup water to pan.

Mix thoroughly bread crumbs, parsley, basil, cheese, orégano, and garlic. Sprinkle evenly over lobster; add salt and pepper to taste. Pour oil over all.

Place on broiler rack about 6 inches below medium flame. Broil about 20 minutes or until lobster meat is tender.

Serve very hot. Serves 2.

## ARAGOSTA MARINARA
### LOBSTER MARINER

| | |
|---|---|
| 1 large lobster (2 lbs.) | 1 tbs. chopped parsley |
| 5 tbs. olive oil | 1 No. 2 can tomatoes |
| 2 whole cloves garlic | 1 sliced onion |
| ½ cup dry sherry | Salt and pepper to taste |

Insert sharp knife between body and tail of lobster to sever spinal cord. Place on back; split. Spread open; cut crosswise for convenience in cooking. The green and coral parts are edible, but be sure to remove the small sac just back of the head. Crack large claws.

Brown garlic and onion in saucepan with olive oil; remove garlic. Add lobster; cover; cook over low flame 10 minutes or until shell is red. Remove lobster; set aside.

Put tomatoes in same pan. Add parsley, salt, and pepper; cover; simmer slowly for 15 minutes.

While sauce is cooking remove lobster from shell and cut into small pieces. When sauce is done add lobster; cover; simmer slowly 10 minutes more. Add sherry.

Serve very hot. Serves 2.

## GAMBERI ALLA MARIO
### SHRIMP MARIO

| | |
|---|---|
| 2 lbs. large fresh shrimp | ¾ cup dry sherry |
| 1 cup flour | ½ cup olive oil |
| 1 large green pepper | Salt and pepper to taste |

Clean and stem pepper; cut into ½-inch pieces.

Clean shrimp and remove shells. Dip in flour and fry in very hot oil about 5 minutes or until brown on both sides. Add salt and pepper to taste. Remove from pan.

Fry pepper in same oil about 10 minutes. When soft, add shrimp; simmer for 2 minutes. Stir. Add sherry; cover; cook 3 minutes over high flame.

Serve with broccoli and buttered rice. Serves 4.

## GAMBERI CON RISO

### SHRIMP WITH RICE

| | |
|---|---|
| 3 cups boiled rice | 2 cups boiled shrimp |
| 4 tbs. olive oil | 1 No. 2 can solid-pack |
| 2 sliced onions | tomatoes |
| 1 tsp. chopped sweet | 2 cups fresh cooked peas |
| basil | ½ cup diced celery |

Salt and pepper to taste

Pour oil in deep saucepan and heat. Add onion and celery; cook about 10 minutes over medium flame, or until soft. Add tomatoes, basil, salt, and pepper. Cook slowly 20 minutes. Stir occasionally. Add peas, shrimp. Cover; cook 5 minutes longer or until shrimp is thoroughly heated.

Place about ½ cup hot rice on individual heated plates; top with shrimp mixture.

Serve very hot. Serves 4 to 6.

## LUMACHE SICILIANA

### SNAILS SICILIAN

| | |
|---|---|
| 2 lbs. snails | 4 tbs. olive oil |
| 1 clove garlic | ½ can tomato paste |
| 1 large chopped onion | 2 cups hot water |
| 1 tbs. chopped parsley | Salt and pepper to taste |

Place snails in large deep pot. Cover with cold water. Rub rim of salt around the inside of pot just below the edge to prevent snails from coming out of water.

Soak for ½ hour. Then wash thoroughly in several waters. Drain well. Use only live snails with heads out of shell.

Pour oil in deep pot. Heat; add onion and garlic; cook slowly 3 minutes or until soft. Remove garlic. Add tomato paste; cook over low flame for 5 minutes, stirring constantly. Add hot water and blend. Add snails; stir; sauté over moderate flame 10 minutes. Add salt and pepper to taste; stir. Add parsley; cover; simmer slowly 20 minutes.

Serve very hot in deep plates with the sauce. (Use small oyster fork or nut pick to extract snail.) Serves 6 to 8.

## OSTRICHE ALLA MARIO

### OYSTERS MARIO

| | |
|---|---|
| 2 doz. large oysters | 1 clove garlic |
| 3 tbs. butter | 1 cup bread crumbs |
| 2 tbs. olive oil | ½ tsp. orégano |
| 2 tbs. chopped parsley | Juice of 1 lemon |
| Salt and pepper to taste | |

Scrub shells; rinse in cold running water. Insert knife blade between edges of shells, cutting through the muscle of oyster. Pry open. Remove from shells.

Rub the half shell with garlic and tiny piece of butter; replace oyster. Sprinkle with salt and pepper.

Mix bread crumbs, olive oil, parsley, and orégano. Sprinkle this mixture on each oyster. Arrange in pan; bake in moderate oven 10 minutes or until edges of oysters curl.

Serve very hot with lemon juice. Serves 4.

## VONGOLI SU PANE ABBRUSTOLITO

### CLAMS ON TOAST

| | |
|---|---|
| 2 doz. clams | ¼ tsp. orégano |
| 2 cloves garlic, chopped | ½ cup water |
| 1 tsp. chopped parsley | 2 cups canned tomatoes |
| 4 slices toast | 4 tbs. olive oil |
| Salt and pepper to taste | |

Scrub clams with stiff brush; rinse in cold running water until all sand is removed. Place in large pot; add water; cover; cook slowly 20 minutes or until shells open. Remove clams from shells.

Place oil in saucepan; heat; brown garlic about 2 minutes. Add tomatoes, parsley, orégano, salt, and pepper. Cook slowly for 20 minutes; stir to prevent sticking. Add steamed clams; cook 1 minute longer.

Place on toast and serve very hot. Serves 4.


## VONGOLI SICILIANA

### STEAMED CLAMS SICILIAN

*2 doz. clams in shells*      *2 tbs. olive oil*
*2 tbs. parsley*             *½ cup water*
*2 cloves garlic*            *Salt and pepper to taste*


Scrub clams with stiff brush; rinse in running water until all sand is removed.

Place garlic, oil, and parsley in large pot; heat 3 minutes. Add water, a little salt and pepper to taste, and clams. Cover; steam over medium flame about 20 minutes or until shells open. Place clams in deep plates.

Serve hot with clam broth. Serves 4.

(Steamed clams may be used on spaghetti with Plain Tomato Sauce. Steam as shown here. Remove from shells; cut clams into small pieces; add to sauce.)

# CHAPTER NINE

# Meats

## Beef

### BISTECCA MILANESE

#### BEEFSTEAK MILANESE

| | |
|---|---|
| 1 sirloin steak (about 3 lbs.) | 3 tbs. butter |
| 1 clove garlic | 2 tbs. olive oil |
| | Salt and pepper to taste |

Sprinkle steak with pepper. Heat skillet. Melt butter; add oil. Brown garlic about 1 minute; remove garlic from pan. Brown steak on each side about 5 minutes over high flame if rare steak is desired, or 7 to 10 minutes for medium rare. Remove from fire. Sprinkle with salt to taste; pour pan gravy over steak while sizzling hot.

Serve immediately. Serves 4 to 6.

### BRACIUOLINI DI MANZO

#### BROILED BEEF ROLLETTES

| | |
|---|---|
| 1½ lbs. top round steak | 2 cloves garlic |
| 3 strips bacon | 2 tsp. chopped parsley |
| 1 large onion, sliced | Salt and pepper to taste |

Have steak sliced very thin (about ¼ inch) and cut into 3-inch squares. Place small piece of garlic, slice of onion, pinch of parsley, and 1-inch piece of bacon in center of each square. Roll carefully so ingredients do not ooze out. Top with small piece of bacon. Fasten each roll together with toothpicks.

74

Place on broiler rack about 5 inches below flame and broil about 5 minutes on each side or until golden brown and tender. Sprinkle with salt and pepper.

Serve very hot. Serves 4 to 6.

## POLPETTE

### MEAT BALLS

| | |
|---|---|
| 1 lb. chopped beef | 6 tbs. olive oil |
| 3 tbs. grated Romano cheese | 3 eggs |
| | 3 slices stale bread |
| 2 tbs. chopped parsley | 1 clove garlic, chopped |
| Salt and pepper to taste | |

Soak bread in water 5 minutes; squeeze dry. Mix thoroughly with meat, slightly beaten eggs, grated Romano cheese, garlic, and parsley. Add salt and pepper to taste. Shape into balls about size of small egg; roll in flour; fry in hot oil about 10 minutes or until golden brown.

Serve very hot with vegetables and salad. May also be served with Spaghetti and Plain Tomato Sauce. Serves 4 to 6.

## FILETTO SICILIANA

### FILET MIGNON SICILIAN

| | |
|---|---|
| 2 lbs. filet mignon | 1/8 lb. butter |
| 1 medium onion, sliced | 1/2 cup marsala (sherry) |
| 2 slices bacon | Salt and pepper to taste |

Have filet sliced 1½ inches thick.

Heat skillet; brown bacon slightly. Add onion; brown 2 minutes. Remove bacon and onion. Brown filet over high flame about 5 minutes on each side. Lower flame; continue frying 5 minutes; add salt and pepper to taste.

Melt butter in separate pan; pour over filet. Add marsala; simmer 2 minutes.

Serve very hot. Serves 4.

# MANZO ALLA MODA

### BEEF À LA MODE

| | |
|---|---|
| *4 lbs. top sirloin or eye round (in 1 piece)* | *1 clove* |
| *2 large carrots, diced* | *2 ozs. butter* |
| *1 tbs. chopped parsley* | *1 cup burgundy* |
| *2 large onions, sliced* | *3 tbs. tomato paste* |
| *2 tbs. olive oil* | *2 cups hot water* |
| | *Salt and pepper to taste* |

Heat olive oil and butter in deep pot. When very hot, brown meat quickly on all sides, about 15 minutes. Add onions, carrots, parsley, and clove; cook for 5 minutes; stir. Dissolve tomato paste in cup of hot water; add. Season to taste. Cover. Cook over low flame for 1¼ hours. Turn meat frequently to prevent scorching.

Add burgundy; cook for 15 minutes longer. Gradually add balance of water; cover; simmer for ¼ hour or until meat is very tender.

Slice; serve very hot. Serves 6 to 8.

# SPIEDINI ALLA ROMANA

### SKEWERED CHOPPED BEEF ROMAN STYLE

*Meat Mixture Ingredients:*

| | |
|---|---|
| *1 lb. chopped beef (top round)* | *½ cup bread crumbs* |
| *2 eggs* | *2 tbs. chopped parsley* |
| *3 tbs. grated Romano cheese* | *1 clove garlic, chopped* |
| | *Salt and pepper to taste* |

Mix all meat ingredients thoroughly. Mold into oblong shapes 2 inches long and 1 inch in diameter. Set aside on platter.

*Other Ingredients:*

| | |
|---|---|
| *1 lb. Mozzarella cheese* | *½ cup flour* |
| *¼ lb. prosciutto (Italian ham)* | *4 slices white bread* |
| | *1 cup bread crumbs* |
| *2 eggs* | *½ cup peanut or olive oil* |

*Salt and pepper to taste*

Have 12 skewers ready. Cut bread, prosciutto, and Mozzarella into 1-inch squares and place on separate plates. Thread each skewer alternately with oblong meat shapes, bread, prosciutto, and Mozzarella. Set aside. Break eggs into deep oblong dish; beat thoroughly. Place bread crumbs and flour on convenient flat board. Dip filled skewer in flour, then in egg, and finally in bread crumbs. Set all aside on platter. Place oil in very large frying pan; when well heated, fry *spiedini* (filled skewers) quickly about 5 minutes on each side or until golden brown but not dry.

Serve on skewers while still sizzling hot. Serves 6.

## *Lamb*

### AGNELLINO AL FORNO

#### ROASTED WHOLE BABY LAMB

| | |
|---|---|
| *1 baby lamb (about 8 lbs.)* | *6 cloves garlic* |
| | *2 whole cloves* |
| *12 strips bacon* | *1 large onion, sliced* |
| *3 large tart apples* | *Salt and pepper to taste* |

Have lamb cleaned, dressed, and slit for stuffing. Rub lightly, inside and out, with salt and pepper. With point of sharp knife make 3 small openings on each side of lamb; insert small pieces of bacon and garlic. Stuff lamb with three whole peeled apples, 4 strips of bacon, and 2 whole cloves. Sew or skewer to prevent stuffing from falling out. Place lamb in roasting pan; put balance of bacon strips and onion over it; brown in hot oven about 30 min-

utes. Baste frequently until whole lamb is golden brown.
Then lower heat; roast about 1½ hours or until tender.
Baste occasionally. If pan becomes dry, add little water.
Serve very hot. Serves 6 to 8.

If preferred, lamb may be broiled over charcoal on a
spit.

At Easter time whole baby lambs may be purchased
from Italian butchers.

## BRACIUOLINI D'AGNELLO

### LAMB ROLLETTES

| | |
|---|---|
| *1¼ lbs. lamb steak* | *4 tbs. olive oil* |
| *2 cloves garlic* | *Pinch of rosemary* |
| *1 large onion, sliced* | *½ cup dry sauterne* |
| *Salt and pepper to taste* | |

Have lamb sliced very thin (about ¼ inch) and cut into
3-inch squares.

Sprinkle lamb lightly with salt and pepper; place small
piece of garlic and slice of onion in center of each square;
roll and fasten with toothpicks.

Heat olive oil in skillet; brown rolls quickly about 5
minutes or until golden color. Sprinkle pinch of rosemary over all; cover; cook slowly about 15 minutes or
until tender. Add sauterne; simmer 3 minutes.

Serve very hot. Serves 4.

## AGNELLO CON RISO

### LAMB WITH RICE

| | |
|---|---|
| *2 lbs. lamb (from leg)* | *¼ cup olive oil* |
| *1 cup rice* | *½ can tomato paste* |
| *1 large onion, sliced* | *1 cup warm water* |
| *Salt and pepper to taste* | |

Have lamb cut into small cubes as for stew.

Pour oil in skillet; heat. Brown lamb slightly for about

8 minutes. Add onion; cover; simmer 5 minutes or until onion is soft. Add salt and pepper.

Blend tomato paste in cup of warm water; add to lamb. Cover; simmer about 45 minutes or until tender.

In the meantime, cook rice about 20 minutes in 2 quarts of boiling water to which ½ teaspoon of salt has been added. Drain in colander; rinse with cup of cold water. Keep hot by placing colander over pot of boiling water.

Arrange rice on hot platter, leaving space in center. Place lamb in hollow; pour sauce over lamb.

Serve very hot. Serves 4 to 6.

## AGNELLO IN UMIDO CON CUCUZZA

### LAMB STEW WITH SQUASH

| | |
|---|---|
| 2 lbs. lean stewing lamb | 1 tsp. orégano |
| 4 tbs. olive oil | 2 large ripe tomatoes |
| 1½ lbs. cucuzza (light green Italian squash) | 1 large onion, sliced |
| | Salt and pepper to taste |

Wash and scrape squash; cut into 1-inch cubes.

Dip tomatoes in boiling water 1 minute; peel.

Have lamb cut into serving pieces.

Pour oil in large saucepan; heat. Add onion; cook about 3 minutes or until soft. Add lamb; cook about 15 minutes or until brown on all sides. Add tomatoes (cut into small pieces). Add orégano, salt and pepper to taste; cover; simmer 20 minutes. Add squash; simmer 10 minutes longer or until squash is tender.

Serve very hot. Serves 4 to 6.

# Pork

## COSTATELLE DI MAIALE

### PORK CHOPS

*4 thick loin pork chops*  *1 tbs. chopped parsley*
*1 cup vinegar*  *1 clove garlic, chopped*
*1 cup bread crumbs*  *1 large egg*
*4 tbs. olive oil*  *½ cup flour*
*Salt and pepper to taste*

Marinate chops in vinegar for about 1 hour in shallow dish. Remove from vinegar. Dry with absorbent paper. Sprinkle with salt and pepper.

Beat egg lightly; blend with 1 tablespoon of cold water. Mix bread crumbs, garlic and parsley, a little salt and pepper.

Roll chops in flour; dip in egg, then in bread crumbs; fry in hot oil for about 5 minutes or until brown on both sides. Lower flame; cover; continue frying slowly for 20 minutes or until well done and tender.

Serve very hot. Serves 4.

## COSTATELLE DI MAIALE CON CAVOLO

### PORK CHOPS AND CABBAGE

*2 lbs. pork chops*  *1 lb. shredded cabbage*
*2 chopped onions*  *4 tbs. olive oil*
*1 clove garlic, chopped*  *1 cup burgundy*
*1 No. 2 can tomatoes*  *Salt and pepper to taste*

Fry onions in hot olive oil for about 3 minutes or until soft. Remove onions; add garlic and pork chops. Turn up flame. Brown chops quickly on both sides about 6 minutes. Transfer chops, garlic, and onions to a deep pot. Add cabbage, tomatoes, salt and pepper to taste; cover tightly; cook slowly for 30 minutes. Add burgundy; continue cooking about 10 minutes, very slowly, or until cabbage and chops are tender.

Serve very hot. Serves 6.

## MAIALINO ARROSTITO

### ROASTED SUCKLING PIG

1 small suckling pig
  (about 10 lbs.)
6 cloves garlic
3 large green apples

3 large oranges
1 tsp. crushed red pepper
  seeds
Salt and pepper to taste

Have suckling cleaned and slit down center for stuffing. Rub lightly (inside and out) with salt and pepper. Peel and quarter oranges and green apples; place inside. Sew or skewer together.

With point of sharp knife make 3 small openings on each side; insert clove of garlic in each.

Sprinkle very lightly with crushed red pepper seeds; roast in very hot oven, watching constantly. When brown, lower heat and roast about 4 hours or until well done. Baste with pan juice from time to time to prevent dryness. When ready to serve, remove garlic; slice thickly.

Serve very hot. Serves 10 to 12.

If preferred, suckling may be roasted on spit over charcoal fire.

Orange and Lemon Salad may be served with suckling.

## *Veal*

## COSTATELLE DI VITELLA CACCIATORA

### VEAL CHOPS HUNTER'S STYLE

1½ lbs. veal chops
1 tbs. butter
5 tbs. olive oil
1 stalk chopped celery
1 medium carrot,
  chopped

1 medium onion,
  chopped
1 tsp. chopped parsley
¾ cup dry sherry
1 tbs. tomato paste
Salt and pepper to taste

Melt butter and oil in hot skillet. Brown chops well on both sides (about 10 minutes). Add all chopped vegetables, salt and pepper to taste; cover; simmer about 10 minutes or until all vegetables are soft. Gradually add sherry into which tomato paste has been well blended. Stir occasionally to prevent burning or sticking. Cover. Simmer over low flame about 20 minutes or until chops are tender. While simmering, if there is insufficient gravy, add 2 tablespoons of warm water.

Serve very hot. Serves 4.


## COTOLETTE ALLA PARMIGIANA

### VEAL CUTLETS PARMESAN

| | |
|---|---|
| *1 lb. veal cutlets* | *½ lb. Mozzarella cheese* |
| *3 tbs. grated Parmesan* | *1 cup bread crumbs* |
| *cheese* | *2 eggs* |
| *6 tbs. olive oil* | *Salt and pepper to taste* |

Beat eggs thoroughly; add salt and pepper. Mix bread crumbs with cheese. Dip cutlets in egg, then in bread crumbs; fry in hot oil about 5 minutes on each side or until golden brown.

Prepare Plain Tomato Sauce #1.

Place browned cutlets in baking pan; pour layer of sauce over them; then place thin slices of Mozzarella over top. Bake in slow oven for 15 minutes or until cheese turns slightly brown.

Serve very hot. Serves 4.


## COTOLETTE DI VITELLA

### VEAL CUTLETS

| | |
|---|---|
| *1 lb. veal cutlets* | *1½ cups bread crumbs* |
| *2 eggs* | *⅓ cup olive oil* |
| *3 tbs. grated Pecorino* | *1 tbs. chopped sweet* |
| *cheese* | *basil* |
| *1 lemon* | *Salt and pepper to taste* |

Mix bread crumbs with cheese, chopped basil, salt and pepper to taste.

Roll cutlets in bread crumbs; dip in egg; roll in bread crumbs.

Heat oil in skillet; brown cutlets quickly on both sides over high flame. Turn down flame; cover; continue frying about 20 minutes or until tender.

Serve very hot with lemon slices. Serves 4.

## OSSI BUCHI ALLA MILANESE

### VEAL SHANKS MILANESE

| | |
|---|---|
| 2 whole veal shanks | 1 medium onion, |
| 3 tbs. butter | chopped |
| 3 tbs. olive oil | 1 tsp. chopped parsley |
| ¼ cup chopped celery | 2 tbs. tomato paste |
| 1 medium carrot, | 1 cup dry sherry |
| chopped | Salt and pepper to taste |

Have veal shanks sawed into 3-inch pieces. Melt butter and oil in deep saucepan; brown veal well on all sides (takes about 10 minutes). Add all chopped vegetables, salt and pepper to taste. Cover; simmer about 10 minutes or until carrots are soft.

Gradually add sherry into which tomato paste has been well blended. Stir occasionally to prevent burning or sticking. Cover; simmer over low flame for about 30 minutes or until veal is tender. While simmering, occasionally add small quantity of water if there is insufficient gravy.

Serve very hot with plain boiled rice. Serves 4.

## ROLLINI DI VITELLA

### VEAL ROLLETTES

| | |
|---|---|
| 1¼ lbs. rump of veal | 1 large clove garlic, |
| 4 ozs. prosciutto (Italian | chopped |
| ham) | 1 large onion, sliced |
| 5 tbs. olive oil | 2 tbs. chopped parsley |
| 2 cup canned tomatoes | Salt and pepper to taste |

Have veal sliced very thinly and cut into 3-inch squares. Chop prosciutto; mix with chopped garlic, parsley, salt, and pepper. Place 1 heaping teaspoon of mixture and slice of onion on each square; roll carefully and tie with string or fasten with toothpicks.

Pour oil in hot skillet; brown rolls quickly on both sides about 5 minutes. Add tomatoes; cover; cook slowly for 30 minutes.

Serve very hot. Serves 4 to 6.

## SCALOPPINE ALLA MARSALA

### VEAL WITH MARSALA

| | |
|---|---|
| *1 lb. thin veal cutlets* | *½ cup marsala (sweet* |
| *1 sliced lemon* | *sherry)* |
| *½ cup flour* | *⅛ lb. butter* |
| | *Salt and pepper to taste* |

Have veal flattened and cut into 4-inch pieces. Roll veal in flour. Heat skillet; melt butter; brown cutlets quickly. Add marsala. Cover; simmer over low flame about 5 minutes or until meat is tender. Sprinkle with salt and pepper.

Serve very hot with lemon slices. Serves 4.

## SPIEDINI ALLA GRIGLIA

### BROILED VEAL ROLLS

| | |
|---|---|
| *1½ lbs. veal rump* | *Pinch of rosemary* |
| *4 ozs. prosciutto (Italian* | *1 cup bread crumbs* |
| *ham)* | *3 tbs. grated Romano* |
| *1 tbs. chopped parsley* | *cheese* |
| *1 clove garlic* | *1 large onion, sliced* |
| *Salt and pepper to taste* | *3 tbs. olive oil* |

Have veal sliced very thinly and cut into 3-inch squares. Chop prosciutto and garlic; mix thoroughly with grated Romano cheese, parsley, salt and pepper. Place 1 teaspoon of mixture in center of each veal square; roll carefully; tie with string or fasten with toothpicks.

Dip each roll in bread crumbs. Alternate 1 roll and 1

slice of onion on skewers until all are used. Brush with
olive oil; sprinkle with rosemary. Place on broiler rack 5
inches below medium flame; broil about 5 minutes or
until golden brown. Turn and brown other side 5 minutes
or until veal is tender.

Serve very hot. Serves 4 to 6.

## VITELLA CON RISO

### VEAL WITH RICE

| | |
|---|---|
| *6 thin veal cutlets* | *2 tbs. grated Romano* |
| *¼ lb. Italian pork* | *cheese* |
| *sausage* | *1 cup canned tomatoes* |
| *2 cups rice* | *2 tbs. chopped parsley* |
| *1 thinly sliced onion* | *¼ cup hot water* |
| *4 ozs. butter* | *1 qt. chicken broth* |
| *2 tbs. olive oil* | *Salt and pepper to taste* |

Fry onion in 2 tablespoons of oil about 3 minutes or
until soft. Add sausage cut up into small pieces; cook 5
minutes. Add washed rice; stir. Add tomatoes and parsley; stir; cook 5 minutes longer. Add chicken broth; lower
flame; cover; cook 30 minutes longer, stirring frequently
to prevent sticking. Add grated cheese; blend well to make
a thick creamy mixture.

Fry cutlets quickly in butter about 10 minutes; add salt
and pepper to taste. When golden brown, add ¼ cup of
hot water to make brown gravy; simmer 5 minutes.

Arrange rice mixture on hot platter; place cutlets on
top; pour gravy over this.

Serve very hot. Serves 6.

## VITELLA CON PEPERONI

### VEAL WITH PEPPERS

| | |
|---|---|
| *1½ lbs. veal rump* | *1 large onion, sliced* |
| *⅔ cup dry sauterne* | *4 large firm green* |
| *5 tbs. olive oil* | *peppers* |
| *3 ozs. butter* | *1 No. 2 can tomatoes* |

*Salt and pepper to taste*

Have veal cut into 1½ inch cubes.

Clean, stem, and seed peppers; cut lengthwise into 1-inch strips.

Melt butter in skillet; brown veal about 10 minutes. Add salt and pepper, tomatoes; cover; simmer about 30 minutes over low flame.

Fry onions and peppers separately in hot oil for about 15 minutes or until tender. Stir to prevent burning. When done, mix with veal. Add sauterne; cover and simmer 15 minutes over very low flame.

Serve very hot. Serves 4 to 6.

## UCCELLI SCAPPATI

### VEAL BIRDS

| | |
|---|---|
| *1½ lbs. veal rump* | *Pinch of rosemary* |
| *4 slices bacon* | *Salt and pepper to taste* |

Have veal cut into 1½-inch cubes. Cut bacon in 1½-inch pieces.

Put skewer through center of each veal cube and piece of bacon. Alternate veal and bacon until skewer is filled. Sprinkle lightly with rosemary. Place on broiler rack about 6 inches below flame. Broil on each side about 6 minutes or until brown and tender. Then sprinkle with salt and pepper.

Serve very hot with pan gravy. Serves 4 to 6.

## Miscellaneous Meats

## CERVELLI IMPANATI

### BREADED BRAINS

| | |
|---|---|
| *2 lbs. calves' brains* | *1 tbs. chopped parsley* |
| *1 cup bread crumbs* | *¼ cup olive or peanut oil* |
| *1 tbs. grated Parmesan cheese* | *Salt and pepper to taste* |

Wash brains thoroughly. Cover with cold water and parboil about 5 minutes. Remove from water; peel off all outer tissues. Cut into 3-inch serving pieces. Blend bread crumbs, parsley, cheese, salt, and pepper. Roll brains in this mixture. Pour oil in frying pan; heat. Fry brains about 5 minutes or until brown on both sides.

Serve very hot with green salad. Serves 4.

## FEGATO CON FUNGHI ALLA GRIGLIA

### BROILED LIVER AND MUSHROOMS

| | |
|---|---|
| *1 lb. calves' liver* | *1 tsp. fresh mint,* |
| *4 tbs. olive oil* | *chopped* |
| *1 sliced onion* | *2 tbs. wine vinegar* |
| *½ lb. mushrooms* | *Salt and pepper to taste* |

Have liver sliced 1 inch thick and cut into 2-inch squares. Clean and remove stems from mushrooms.

Alternate a piece of liver, a mushroom cap, and slice of onion on 8 skewers until all ingredients are used.

Mix oil, vinegar, and mint thoroughly; brush liver and mushrooms on both sides. Place on broiler rack about 5 inches below flame. Broil three minutes on each side or until light brown. Salt and pepper to taste. Brush with remaining liquid; broil 1 minute longer and remove from skewers. If preferred, may be served on skewers.

Serve sizzling hot. Serves 4.

## FEGATO CON VINO

### LIVER WITH CLARET

| | |
|---|---|
| *1½ lbs. calves' liver* | *½ cup claret* |
| *2 sliced onions* | *½ cup flour* |
| *6 tbs. olive oil* | *Salt and pepper to taste* |

Have liver sliced ¾ inch thick. Sprinkle lightly with salt and pepper; roll in flour.

Pour oil in frying pan; heat. Brown onion about 3 minutes or until soft. Remove onion.

Fry liver quickly about 3 minutes on each side over high flame. Replace onion; add claret; turn flame very high for 1 minute. Remove from fire; serve immediately. Serves 4.

## POLPETTONE

### MEAT LOAF

| | |
|---|---|
| *½ lb. chopped beef* | *1 hard-boiled egg* |
| *½ lb. chopped lean pork* | *3 tbs. grated Romano* |
| *1 tbs. chopped parsley* | *cheese* |
| *4 tbs. olive oil* | *¼ lb. Mozzarella* |
| *2 eggs* | *Salt and pepper to taste* |

Mix meat, eggs, cheese, parsley, salt, and pepper thoroughly.

Pour 2 tablespoons of oil in bottom of small deep oblong baking dish. Put half of meat mixture in it. Slice Mozzarella and hard-boiled egg. Place layer of each over meat. Cover with balance of meat mixture to form a loaf. Pour 2 tablespoons of oil over loaf; bake in moderate oven about 25 minutes or until golden brown but not dry.

Slice and serve very hot. Serves 4.

## POLPETTONE CON PATATE

### MEAT LOAF WITH POTATO FILLING

| | |
|---|---|
| *1 lb. chopped lean beef* | *½ cup grated Parmesan* |
| *or* | *cheese* |
| *half beef and half veal* | *½ cup water* |
| *1 cup bread crumbs* | *½ lb. Mozzarella cheese* |
| *1 tbs. chopped parsley* | *4 tbs. olive oil* |
| *2 eggs* | *1 small onion, chopped* |
| *2 cups mashed potatoes* | *Salt and pepper to taste* |

Blend 1 teaspoon of parsley with mashed potatoes.

Mix meat, bread crumbs, water, parsley, grated cheese, eggs, onions, salt, and pepper very thoroughly.

Brush a 10-inch Pyrex baking dish with 1 tablespoon of olive oil. Sprinkle lightly with 2 tablespoons of bread crumbs.

Place half of meat mixture in dish; alternate a layer of mashed potatoes and a layer of sliced Mozzarella. Top with balance of meat. Close edges firmly so potatoes do not show or ooze out. Brush with balance of oil. Bake 25 minutes in moderate oven until meat is golden brown but not dry.

Turn over on hot platter; slice and serve very hot. Serves 6.

## POLPETTONE CON RICOTTA

### MEAT LOAF WITH RICOTTA

| | |
|---|---|
| *1 lb. chopped lean beef* | *½ cup grated Romano* |
| *or* | *cheese* |
| *half beef and half veal* | *½ cup water* |
| *1 cup bread crumbs* | *1 small onion, chopped* |
| *3 eggs* | *¾ lb. ricotta (Italian cot-* |
| *4 tbs. olive oil* | *tage cheese)* |
| *1½ tbs. chopped parsley* | *Salt and pepper to taste* |

Mix meat, bread crumbs, water, 1 tablespoon of parsley, grated cheese, 2 eggs, onion, salt, and pepper very thoroughly.

Mix ricotta, 1 egg, ½ tablespoon of parsley, and pinch of salt until well blended.

Brush 10-inch Pyrex baking dish with 2 tablespoons of oil. Sprinkle lightly with 2 additional tablespoons of bread crumbs. Place half of meat mixture in dish. Spread ricotta mixture over this and top with balance of meat. Close edges firmly so ricotta does not ooze out. Brush with balance of oil. Bake about 25 minutes in hot oven or until meat is golden brown but not dry and ricotta is firm.

Turn over on heated platter. Slice and serve very hot. Serves 6.

## ROGNONI AL VINO ROSSO

### KIDNEYS WITH BURGUNDY

*4 lamb kidneys*          *2 tsp. chopped parsley or*
*1 sliced onion*               *chopped sweet basil*
*2 ozs. butter*           *½ cup burgundy*
*1 pt. boiling water*     *Salt and pepper to taste*

Have all fat and outer membrane removed. Cut kidneys into ½-inch slices. Cover with cold salted water. Allow to stand for 1 hour. Drain. Clean kidneys well by placing in saucepan and pouring 1 pint of boiling water over them; drain thoroughly.

Melt butter in shallow saucepan. Place kidneys and onions in hot butter; cover; simmer for 20 minutes or until tender. Add salt and pepper to taste. Pour burgundy over kidneys; simmer 3 minutes. Sprinkle with parsley or basil.

Serve very hot. Serves 4.

## SALSICCIA ALLA GRIGLIA

### BROILED SAUSAGE

*2½ lbs. Italian sausage*

Place sausage on broiler rack 6 inches below medium flame. While broiling, prick in several places with fork to allow fat to escape. Broil 30 minutes or until well done and golden brown on all sides.

Serve very hot with sautéed green peppers and salad. Serves 4 to 6.

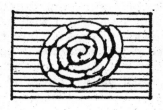

# SALSICCIA CON VINO ROSSO

### SAUSAGE WITH BURGUNDY

*2½ lbs. Italian sausage          2 cups cold water*
*½ cup burgundy*

Place cold water and sausage in skillet; boil briskly 3 minutes. Lower flame; prick sausage with fork, allowing fat to escape. Cook about 20 minutes or until all water evaporates and sausage is brown. Turn; brown other side 10 minutes or until well done. Gradually add burgundy; cover; simmer 5 minutes.

Serve very hot with salad. Serves 4 to 6.


# TRIPPA MILANESE

### TRIPE MILANESE

*2 lbs. honeycomb tripe*          *2 ozs. butter*
*2 cups boiled rice*              *¼ cup grated Parmesan*
*1 cup water*                     *cheese*
*½ cup tomato paste*              *Salt and pepper to taste*

Have tripe cut into 1-inch squares. Clean thoroughly by rinsing in cold water. Place tripe in 4 quarts of cold water in deep pot; cover; boil slowly about 2 hours or until tender. Drain.

Melt butter in saucepan. Add tripe; sauté for 5 minutes over low flame. Blend tomato paste in 1 cup of water; pour over tripe. Cover; simmer 30 minutes or until tripe is very tender. Blend in hot rice and cheese.

Serve very hot. Serves 4 to 6.

## UMIDO DI CARNE
### MEAT STEW

| | |
|---|---|
| 1 lb. lean beef | ½ cup diced celery |
| 1 lb. lean lamb | 1 No. 2 can tomatoes |
| 4 tbs. olive oil | 3 sprigs parsley |
| 1 clove garlic | 3 large potatoes, |
| 2 whole cloves | quartered |
| 1 tbs. butter | 1 chopped onion |
| ½ cup burgundy | Salt and pepper to taste |

Have meat cut into 1½-inch cubes. Fry chopped onion
and garlic in olive oil and butter about 5 minutes or until
soft. Transfer to large saucepan. Add meat; brown well
for about 10 minutes. Add burgundy gradually; stir to
prevent burning. Add salt, pepper, tomatoes, celery, parsley, and cloves. Cover; cook for ½ hour over low flame.
Add potatoes; continue cooking for about 20 minutes or
until meat and potatoes are tender.

Serve very hot. Serves 6 to 8.

# CHAPTER TEN

# Vegetables and Salads

## Vegetables

### BROCCOLI CON OLIVE

#### BROCCOLI WITH OLIVES

Follow same recipe as for Broccoli Siciliana, but omit lemon and anchovy. Add ½ cup of chopped black Italian olives. Heat thoroughly and serve very hot.

### BROCCOLI ALLA SICILIANA

#### BROCCOLI SICILIAN

| | |
|---|---|
| *1 bunch broccoli* | *4 tbs. olive oil* |
| *1 clove garlic* | *1 lemon* |
| *3 filets of anchovy* | *Salt and pepper to taste* |

Clean and wash broccoli. Cut into medium-sized pieces. Cook in rapidly boiling salted water for 10 minutes. Drain. Put olive oil, garlic, and anchovies (cut into small pieces) in saucepan. Heat thoroughly. Add broccoli and ¼ cup of warm water. Simmer for about 10 minutes or until tender. Flavor with lemon juice and serve very hot.
Serves 4.

## CAPONATA ALA SICILIANA

### DICED EGGPLANT SICILIAN

| | |
|---|---|
| 2 medium-sized | 2 ozs. capers (washed) |
| eggplants | 1 tbs. pine nuts |
| 2 sliced onions | 2 tbs. sugar |
| 1 cup diced celery | 4 tbs. wine vinegar |
| 1 No. 2 can strained | ½ cup olive oil |
| tomatoes | Salt and pepper to taste |

Wash eggplants; dry with absorbent paper. Dice into 1-inch cubes. Fry in very hot oil about 10 minutes or until soft and slightly browned. Remove eggplant and put in large saucepan.

Fry onion in same oil about 3 minutes; add a little oil if necessary. When onions are golden brown, add tomatoes and celery; simmer about 15 minutes or until celery is tender. Add capers and nuts. Add this mixture to eggplant.

Dissolve sugar in vinegar; add salt and pepper to taste; heat slightly. Add to eggplant; cover; simmer about 20 minutes over very low flame. Stir occasionally to distribute flavor evenly. When done, place in bowl. Cool.

May be used as a side dish with meat or fowl; also as a sandwich filling or antipasto. Keeps for days in refrigerator. Serves 6 to 8.

## CARCIOFI ARROSTITI

### ROASTED ARTICHOKES

| | |
|---|---|
| 6 medium-sized | 6 tbs. olive oil |
| artichokes | 3 tbs. chopped parsley |
| 2 cloves garlic, chopped | ½ cup water |
| | Salt and pepper to taste |

Remove outer leaves from artichokes. Cut off stems. Tap artichokes on table to spread leaves open. Wash; drain for few minutes.

Mix garlic, parsley, and a little salt and pepper (a

pinch of pepper and about ¼ teaspoon of salt). Divide mixture in 6 parts. Distribute one portion between the leaves of each artichoke. Then close leaves. Place upright in saucepan so they fit snugly. Add half of olive oil to bottom of pan; pour other half over the artichokes.

Cook over high flame for about 5 minutes. Watch carefully to prevent burning. Add water; lower flame a little; cook uncovered about 8 minutes or until water evaporates. Then add a little more water; cover pan; cook slowly about 20 minutes or until tender. Test by pulling outer leaf. If it comes off easily, artichokes are done.

Serve hot, as side dish. Serves 6.

## CARCIOFI BOLLITI

### BOILED ARTICHOKES

6 medium-sized                2 qts. water
   artichokes                 1½ tsp. salt
                1 slice lemon

Remove tough outer leaves from artichokes; cut off stems. Wash. Drain.

Place artichokes in 2 quarts of rapidly boiling salted water. Add lemon slice. Boil about 20 minutes or until tender. Test by pulling outer leaf. If it comes out easily, artichokes are done.

Serve hot or cold with French or Italian dressing. Serves 6.

## CARCIOFI FRITTI

### FRIED ARTICHOKES

12 boiled artichoke           6 tbs. olive oil
   hearts (fresh or           1 cup bread crumbs
   canned                     1 tbs. chopped parsley
2 eggs                        Salt and pepper to taste

Sprinkle artichoke hearts with salt and pepper. Mix parsley with bread crumbs. Beat eggs slightly.

Dip artichoke hearts in egg; roll in bread crumbs. Fry in hot olive oil about 3 minutes on each side or until golden brown.

Serve very hot. Serves 6.

## CARCIOFI IMBOTTITI ALLA SICILIANA

### STUFFED ARTICHOKES SICILIAN

*4 large artichokes*
*1 cup bread crumbs*
*4 tbs. grated*
    *Caciocavallo cheese*

*4 chopped anchovy filets*
*2 cloves garlic, chopped*
*2 tbs. parsley, chopped*
*6 tbs. olive oil*
*Salt and pepper to taste*

Cut off stems and about ½ inch tips of artichokes. Remove tough outer leaves. Wash carefully. Tap on table to spread leaves open. Shake out all water.

Mix thoroughly bread crumbs, grated cheese, chopped parsley, anchovies, garlic, salt, and pepper. Divide mixture into 4 parts; distribute one portion between the leaves of each artichoke. Then close. Place upright in saucepan to fit snugly. Pour 1 tablespoon of olive oil over each artichoke. Put remaining oil in saucepan. Add 1 cup of water. Cover tightly; cook slowly for ½ hour or until tender.

Test by pulling outer leaf. If it comes out easily, artichokes are done. Watch water carefully; if it evaporates, add a little more.

Serves 4.

## CAVOLO IMBOTTITO

### STUFFED CABBAGE

*1 tender cabbage*
    *(about 3 lbs.)*
*1 cup chopped cooked*
    *spinach*
*1 tbs. chopped parsley*
*5 tbs. olive oil*

*½ lb. chopped cooked*
    *beef*
*½ cup grated Romano*
    *cheese*
*2 eggs*
*Salt and pepper to taste*

Clean and boil whole cabbage in salted water for 5 minutes. Drain thoroughly.

Beat eggs slightly. Mix very thoroughly all other ingredients except oil.

Spread leaves carefully; insert some of stuffing in center of leaves until all is used. Then close by tying twine around cabbage to prevent stuffing from falling out.

Put in baking dish; add olive oil. Bake in medium oven for 25 minutes or until cabbage is tender. Add ½ cup of hot water if pan is dry.

Serves 6.

## CICORIA FINA AGLIATA

### DANDELION SAUTÉED WITH GARLIC

2 lbs. fresh dandelion
  greens
4 tbs. olive oil

2 cloves garlic, chopped
Salt and pepper to taste

Clean and wash dandelion greens thoroughly; cut in half.

Heat olive oil and garlic in saucepan. Add dandelion; salt and pepper to taste. Cook about 12 minutes or until tender. If too dry, add ¼ cup of hot water. Usually sufficient water is retained in vegetable; additional water is not necessary.

Serve very hot; enough for 4.

## ESCAROLA IMBOTTITA

### STUFFED ESCAROLE

2 medium heads escarole
5 ripe olives, chopped
4 filets of anchovy,
  chopped
1 tbs. pine nuts

1 tbs. seeded raisins
½ lb. chopped beef
½ cup bread crumbs
1 tbs. chopped parsley
5 tbs. olive oil

Salt and pepper to taste

Fry beef about 10 minutes or until slightly browned in 2 tablespoons of olive oil. Remove from fire. Add nuts, raisins, chopped olives, bread crumbs, chopped anchovy, parsley, very little salt and pepper. Mix thoroughly. If too dry, add 2 tablespoons of hot water.

Remove outer leaves from escarole. Wash heads thoroughly. Flatten them out. Place half of mixture in center. Close heads and tie with white twine so stuffing does not fall out.

Arrange in pan. Pour balance of oil over all. Cover tightly and cook over low flame about 20 minutes or until escarole is tender. Turn occasionally to avoid burning. If needed, add another tablespoon of olive oil.

May be used as an entrée. Serves 4.

## ESCAROLA SAUTÉ

### SAUTÉED ESCAROLE

2 lbs. escarole
1 clove garlic

4 tbs. olive oil
Salt and pepper to taste

Remove tough or faded outer leaves. Separate well. Wash thoroughly. Drain. Cut leaves in half. Heat oil in large saucepan; brown garlic, then remove. Add escarole and cook over medium flame for about 20 minutes or until tender. Salt and pepper to taste.

Serve very hot. Serves 4 to 6.

## FAGIOLINI SAUTÉ

### SAUTÉED STRING BEANS

1 lb. string beans
1 clove garlic

2 tbs. olive oil
Salt and pepper to taste

Clean and cut string beans in half. Wash again; drain. Cook in 1 quart of rapidly boiling salted water for about 20 minutes or until as tender as desired. Drain. Brown garlic in hot oil in saucepan for 2 minutes. Remove garlic. Add beans; sauté about 5 minutes.

Serve immediately when very hot. Serves 4 to 6.

## FUNGHI ALLA PARMIGIANA

### MUSHROOMS PARMESAN

*1½ lbs. mushrooms*
*2 tbs. chopped parsley*
*2 cloves garlic, chopped*
*4 tbs. grated Parmesan*
  *cheese*

*¼ cup olive oil*
*½ tsp. orégano*
*¾ cup bread crumbs*
*Salt and pepper to taste*

Clean mushrooms. Place in baking dish which has been brushed with 1 tablespoon of olive oil. Sprinkle with parsley, garlic, orégano, half of bread crumbs, and grated cheese. Add salt and pepper to taste. Pour balance of oil over this; sprinkle with balance of bread crumbs. Bake in moderate oven about 25 minutes or until mushrooms are tender. Add ¼ cup of hot water if mushrooms become too dry; bake 5 minutes longer.
Serve very hot. Serves 6.

## FUNGHI IMBOTTITI

### STUFFED MUSHROOMS

*1 lb. large mushrooms*
*3 tbs. grated Parmesan*
  *cheese*
*1 clove garlic, chopped*
*1 small onion, chopped*

*1 cup bread crumbs*
*1 tbs. chopped parsley*
*2 tbs. melted butter*
*6 tbs. olive oil*
*Salt and pepper to taste*

Clean and remove stems from mushrooms. Mix thoroughly bread crumbs, cheese, parsley, butter, garlic, onion, salt, and pepper. Fill mushroom caps.
Pour 2 tablespoons of oil in bottom of baking pan. Place mushrooms in pan, stuffed side up. Pour balance of oil equally over all mushrooms. Bake about 20 minutes in medium oven. When mushrooms are tender and tops are brown, remove from oven.
Serve very hot. Enough for 4 to 6.

## MELENZANA FRITTA

### FRIED EGGPLANT

| | |
|---|---|
| *1 large eggplant* | *¾ cup peanut oil* |
| *2 ozs. grated Parmesan* | *2 tbs. chopped parsley* |
| *cheese* | *Salt and pepper to taste* |

Peel and cut eggplant crosswise into ½-inch slices. Place in bowl; cover with hot water and let stand for 5 minutes. Drain; dry with absorbent paper. Fry in hot oil about 3 minutes on each side or until soft and light brown. Sprinkle with salt and pepper to taste. Remove from frying pan. Arrange on heated platter; sprinkle with chopped parsley and grated cheese.

Serve very hot. Serves 4.

## MELENZANA ALLA PARMIGIANA

### EGGPLANT PARMESAN

| | |
|---|---|
| *1 large eggplant* | *½ cup olive or peanut* |
| *2 cups bread crumbs* | *oil* |
| *1 tbs. chopped parsley* | *½ lb. Mozzarella cheese* |
| *2 cloves garlic, chopped* | *1 No. 2 can tomatoes* |
| *2 tbs. tomato paste* | *Salt and pepper to taste* |
| *½ cup grated Parmesan cheese* | |

Blend tomato paste with tomatoes. Add 2 tablespoons of olive oil, a pinch of salt, and simmer in saucepan for 30 minutes.

Wash, dry, and slice eggplant crosswise into ½-inch slices. Place in bowl; cover with hot water and let stand for 5 minutes. Drain; dry with absorbent paper. Fry in hot oil about 3 minutes on each side or until soft and light brown. Sprinkle with salt and pepper to taste. Remove from pan.

Mix bread crumbs, cheese, parsley, garlic, a pinch of salt and pepper. Then place one layer of eggplant in bottom of baking dish; sprinkle with bread-crumb mixture; pour some tomato sauce over this. Alternate layers until all ingredients are used. Top with Mozzarella sliced thin. Bake for 10 minutes in moderate oven, or until Mozzarella turns slightly brown.

Serve very hot. Serves 4 to 6. May be used as an entrée.


## MELENZANA ALLA GRIGLIA

### BROILED EGGPLANT

*1 large eggplant*  
*1 cup Plain Tomato*  
*Sauce #1*  
*½ cup Italian Salad*  
*Dressing*  
*Salt and pepper to taste*  
*2 ozs. grated Pecorino cheese*

Peel and cut eggplant crosswise into ¾-inch slices. Marinate in dressing for 30 minutes. Broil under low flame for 5 minutes; turn and broil other side 5 minutes or until medium brown and soft. Arrange on Pyrex platter in layers; alternate hot tomato sauce and eggplant. Top with sauce. Sprinkle with grated cheese. Place under broiler for 2 minutes to brown cheese quickly.

Serves 4 to 6.


## PEPERONI ARROSTITI

### ROASTED PEPPERS

*6 large firm green*  
*peppers*  
*1 clove garlic, chopped*  
*4 tbs. olive oil*  
*1 tbs. vinegar*  
*Salt and pepper to taste*

Wash and dry peppers. Put on broiler rack 6 inches below medium flame. Broil about 10 minutes or until brown on both sides. Watch very carefully, turning frequently to prevent burning. When peppers are soft, remove and cool. Peel off brown skin; take out stems and seeds; cut lengthwise in 2-inch strips.

Mix oil, vinegar, and garlic very thoroughly. Add salt and pepper to taste. Place peppers in deep dish; pour mixture over them. Allow to marinate until ready to serve.

Serve cold with meat or fish. Serves 4.

## PEPERONI FRITTI

### FRIED PEPPERS

*8 large firm green*          *6 tbs. olive oil*
*  peppers*                  *1 clove garlic, halved*
              *Salt and pepper to taste*

Wash and dry peppers. Remove stems and seeds. Cut lengthwise into 1½-inch strips. Use large frying pan. Heat oil and garlic slightly. Add peppers, salt and pepper to taste. Fry over high flame for about 5 minutes. Watch carefully to prevent burning. Stir occasionally. When slightly brown, lower flame; cover; cook for about 15 minutes or until soft.

Serve hot with sausage or veal. Serves 6.

## PEPERONI IMBOTTITI

### STUFFED PEPPERS

*6 large firm green*          *2 tbs. tomato paste*
*  peppers*                  *½ cup cooked chopped*
*3 filets of anchovy,*          *  meat*
*  chopped*                  *½ cup boiled rice*
*5 tbs. olive oil*            *½ cup bread crumbs*
*3 tbs. grated Romano*        *1 small onion, chopped*
*  cheese*                    *1 cup hot water*
*1 tbs. chopped parsley*       *1 egg*
              *Salt and pepper to taste*

Blend tomato paste in hot water.

Wash peppers; remove stems and seeds. Combine all other ingredients except oil and tomato paste. Mix thoroughly. Stuff peppers.

Arrange in baking dish; pour oil over them. Bake in hot oven 15 minutes. Add blended tomato paste; continue baking for 15 minutes or until peppers are tender.

Serve very hot. Serves 6.

# SPARAGI PARMIGIANA

## ASPARAGUS PARMESAN

*1 bunch fresh asparagus*          *⅛ lb. butter*
   *(about 2 lbs.)*                *Salt and pepper to taste*
            *2 ozs. grated Parmesan cheese*

Wash asparagus. Cut off tough ends; remove scales. Scrub stalks thoroughly or peel off outer skin. Cook in rapidly boiling salted water about 20 minutes or until partially tender. Place in baking dish. Melt butter; pour over asparagus; pepper lightly. Sprinkle generously with grated Parmesan cheese. Place in hot oven for about 10 minutes or until cheese turns slightly brown.

Serve very hot. Serves 4.

# SPINACI AFFOGATI

## STEAMED SPINACH

*2 lbs. fresh spinach*          *1 clove garlic*
*4 tbs. olive oil*              *Salt and pepper to taste*

Clean and wash spinach thoroughly. Heat olive oil and garlic in saucepan; add spinach, salt and pepper to taste. Cook about 12 minutes or until tender. If too dry, add ¼ cup of hot water. Usually sufficient water is retained in spinach; additional water is unnecessary.

Serves 6 to 8.

# ZUCCHINI DOLCE E AGRO

## SQUASH SWEET AND SOUR

*6 medium-sized zucchini*          *1 tbs. sugar*
   *(Italian squash)*              *1 tbs. chopped sweet*
*½ cup peanut oil*                    *basil*
*3 tbs. wine vinegar*              *Salt and pepper to taste*

Wash and scrape zucchini lightly. Cut into lengthwise slices about ⅜ inch thick. Fry in oil, about 3 minutes on each side or until slightly brown. Sprinkle with salt and pepper. When done, remove from frying pan and place in deep dish.

Mix thoroughly sugar and vinegar; add to remaining oil in frying pan. Boil slowly for 2 minutes. Pour this over the zucchini. Sprinkle with chopped basil.

Serve very hot or cold. Serves 4.

## ZUCCHINI FRITTI

### FRIED SQUASH

| | |
|---|---|
| *3 zucchini (about 2 in.* | *2 tbs. chopped parsley* |
| *in diameter, 8 in. long)* | *2 ozs. grated Romano* |
| *½ cup peanut oil* | *cheese* |
| *Salt and pepper to taste* | |

Select 3 firm zucchini. Wash and scrape lightly. Cut crosswise into ½-inch slices. Fry in hot oil for about 3 minutes or until slightly brown and soft. Sprinkle with salt and pepper. When done, place on hot platter. Sprinkle each slice with chopped parsley and grated cheese.

Serve hot. Serves 6 to 8.

## *Salads*

## INSALATA D'ARANCIO E LIMONE

### ORANGE AND LEMON SALAD

| | |
|---|---|
| *3 large lemons* | *3 large oranges* |
| *1 head lettuce* | *4 tbs. olive oil* |
| *½ tsp. chopped fresh* | *Salt and pepper to taste* |
| *mint* | |

Quarter unpeeled fruit or cut into small sections, as preferred. Place in salad bowl. Sprinkle lightly with mint, salt, and pepper. Pour olive oil over fruit and mix thoroughly. Place on lettuce leaves and serve.

Serves 6.

## INSALATA DI CALAMAI

### SQUID SALAD

| | |
|---|---|
| 2 lbs. squids | 4 tbs. olive oil |
| 1 clove garlic | Juice of 1 large lemon |
| 1 tbs. fresh mint, | Salt and pepper to taste |
| chopped | |

Have squids cleaned. Cut into small pieces about 2 inches long. Boil in 2 quarts of water about 30 minutes or until tender. Drain well. Add salt.

Blend ingredients well. Pour over squid. Marinate in cool place for several hours.

Serve cold on lettuce leaves. Serves 4 to 6.

## INSALATA DI CICORIA FINA

### DANDELION SALAD

| | |
|---|---|
| 1 lb. dandelion greens | 1 clove garlic |
| 4 tbs. olive oil | 2 tbs. wine vinegar |
| 12 ripe olives | Salt and pepper to taste |

Remove undesirable leaves. Cut dandelion into 2-inch pieces; wash thoroughly in cold water. Drain; dry with absorbent paper. Chill in refrigerator about 10 minutes.

Rub wooden salad bowl with garlic; place dandelion in bowl. Pour olive oil and vinegar over leaves. Add salt and pepper to taste; add olives. Mix and toss thoroughly.

Serve immediately. Serves 4 to 6.

## INSALATA D'ESCAROLA

### ESCAROLE SALAD

| | |
|---|---|
| 1 medium head escarole | 4 leaves fresh sweet |
| 2 tbs. wine vinegar | basil, chopped |
| 6 tbs. olive oil | Salt and pepper to taste |

Remove outside leaves. Wash thoroughly. Crisp in cold water for 15 minutes. Cut into 1-inch pieces. Drain; dry with absorbent paper.

Place escarole in salad bowl. Mix oil, vinegar, basil, salt, and pepper separately. Pour over salad. Toss and mix well.

Serves 4 to 6.

## INSALATA DI FAGIOLINI

### STRING BEAN SALAD

| | |
|---|---|
| *1 lb. string beans* | *4 tbs. olive oil* |
| *1 clove garlic* | *2 tbs. vinegar* |
| *2 qts. water* | *Salt and pepper to taste* |

Cut off tips of beans. Wash thoroughly. Place in rapidly boiling salted water. Cook about 20 minutes or until tender. Drain. Cut in half. Place in wooden salad bowl. Add oil, vinegar, garlic, salt and pepper to taste. Mix thoroughly.

May be served warm; otherwise chill in refrigerator 15 minutes. Serves 6.

## INSALATA DI FINOCCHIO, POMODORO E CICORIA

### FENNEL, TOMATO, AND CHICORY SALAD

| | |
|---|---|
| *1 head finocchio* | *6 tbs. olive oil* |
| *(fennel)* | *1 clove garlic* |
| *2 large firm tomatoes* | *2 tbs. wine vinegar* |
| *1 small head chicory* | *Salt and pepper to taste* |

Remove outer leaves from finocchio and chicory. Wash thoroughly. Cut finocchio in thin slices. Cut chicory into 2-inch pieces. Wash thoroughly again. Dry with absorbent paper. Quarter tomatoes.

Rub large salad bowl with garlic. Add finocchio, chicory, tomatoes, salt and pepper to taste. Blend oil and vinegar separately; pour over salad. Toss and mix thoroughly. Chill in refrigerator for 5 minutes.

Serve on individual salad plates. Serves 6 to 8.

## INSALATA DI LATTUGA ROMANA

### ROMAINE SALAD

*1 medium head romaine*        *1 large sweet onion*
*6 tbs. olive oil*             *2 tbs. wine vinegar*
              *Salt and pepper to taste*

Remove outside leaves from romaine. Wash thoroughly. Crisp in cold water for 15 minutes. Cut into 1-inch pieces. Drain; dry with absorbent paper. Slice onion.

Place romaine and onion in salad bowl. Mix oil, vinegar, salt, and pepper separately. Pour over salad. Toss and mix well.

Serves 4 to 6.

## INSALATA MISTA

### MIXED SALAD

*½ head escarole*            *6 tbs. olive oil*
*½ head chicory*             *1 clove garlic*
*¼ lb. dandelion greens*     *2 tbs. wine vinegar*
*¼ medium-sized*             *Salt and pepper to taste*
*  cucumber*

Peel and slice cucumber thinly. Remove outer leaves from all greens. Cut into 2-inch lengths. Wash thoroughly in cold water. Drain; dry.

Rub salad bowl with garlic. Put in mixed greens and sliced cucumber. Blend oil, vinegar, salt, and pepper and pour over salad. Toss and mix thoroughly.

Serves 6 to 8.

## INSALATA DI PATATE E UOVA

### POTATO AND EGG SALAD

*4 large cold boiled*        *6 tbs. olive oil*
*  potatoes*                 *3 tbs. wine vinegar*
*4 hard-boiled eggs*         *½ cup chopped celery*
*2 tsp. chopped parsley*     *Salt and pepper to taste*

Cut potatoes into small cubes. Quarter eggs. Place in wooden salad bowl. Add celery and parsley. Blend oil and vinegar separately; add to salad. Sprinkle with salt and pepper. Thoroughly chill in refrigerator before serving.
Serves 6.


## INSALATA DI POMODORO CON OREGANO

### TOMATO SALAD WITH ORÉGANO DRESSING

*4 large firm tomatoes*        *4 tbs. olive oil*
*1 tbs. orégano*               *Salt and pepper to taste*

Wash, dry, and slice tomatoes; arrange on platter. Sprinkle with salt, pepper, and orégano. Pour olive oil over all. Chill in refrigerator.
Serves 4.


## Salad Dressings

These dressings may be used with all green salads, including romaine, endive, escarole, chicory, and dandelion.


### SWEET BASIL DRESSING

*3 tbs. chopped sweet*         *½ cup olive oil*
*   basil*      *1 clove garlic*
*4 tbs. wine vinegar*          *Salt and pepper to taste*

Blend all ingredients thoroughly. Place in jar; keep in cool place, *not cold.* Allow to stand several hours before using. Use as needed.
Excellent on all vegetable salads.

## ITALIAN SALAD DRESSING

*½ cup olive oil*            *1 clove garlic, halved*
*¼ tsp. salt*                *½ tsp. dry mustard*
                  *4 tbs. wine vinegar*

Mix mustard, salt, and garlic thoroughly. Add vinegar; stir. Add oil; stir vigorously until all ingredients are well blended. Keep in jar in cold place. Use as needed. This may also be used as a basic recipe for other salad dressings.

## GORGONZOLA CHEESE DRESSING

Use same ingredients and measurements as for Italian Salad Dressing. Add 2 ounces of crumbled **Gorgonzola** cheese. Stir thoroughly before using.

## ROQUEFORT CHEESE DRESSING

Use same ingredients and measurements as for Italian Salad Dressing. Add 2 ounces of crumbled Roquefort cheese. Stir thoroughly before using.

# CHAPTER ELEVEN

# Game and Fowl

## Game

### CERVO ALLA MARIO

#### VENISON MARIO

| | |
|---|---|
| 4 lbs. venison | 2 cloves |
| 2 cups vinegar | 2 tbs. chopped parsley |
| 4 cups cold water | 2 cloves garlic |
| 1 cup sherry | 2 large onions |
| 4 strips salt pork or | 2 large carrots, diced |
|    bacon | 3 tbs. flour |

Salt and pepper to taste

Blend vinegar and water; bring to a boil. Turn off flame; add carrots, garlic, parsley, clove, and 1 onion. Allow to cool. Put venison in this mixture. Let it marinate for 24 hours in a cold place.

Now prepare as follows:

Take venison out of mixture; dry it with absorbent paper. Sprinkle with salt and pepper. Rub with flour. Put 4 strips of salt pork or bacon over venison. Add whole onion and place in baking pan.

Brown venison on both sides in hot oven (this takes about 30 minutes). Then add all vegetables in which venison marinated; add a little of the liquid. Lower heat to moderate oven. Baste occasionally with liquid, using enough to make a gravy. Roast for about 1½ hours or until tender. Then add sherry; simmer slowly for 10 more minutes.

Serve very hot. Serves 6.

## · CONIGLIO FRITTO

### FRIED RABBIT

*1 rabbit ( 3 or 4 lbs.)*     *1 lemon*
*6 slices bacon*     *2 tbs. salt*
*⅛ lb. butter*     *Pinch of sage*
*Salt and pepper to taste*

Have rabbit cleaned and cut into serving pieces. Place in deep dish. Cover with cold water; add 2 tablespoons salt. Let stand in cold place for about 4 hours. Remove. Wash in cold water; dry with absorbent paper.

Place bacon in skillet; brown slowly. Remove bacon; add butter and sage. Sprinkle rabbit lightly with pepper and very little salt to taste. Fry in hot pan for about 15 minutes or until golden brown. Lower flame; cover; continue frying about ½ hour or until tender.

Serve very hot with green salad and lemon slices. Serves 4 to 6.

## CONIGLIO AL FORNO

### ROASTED RABBIT

*1 rabbit (3-4 lbs.)*     *1 tbs. salt*
*2 sliced onions*     *3 sliced carrots*
*6 slices bacon*     *2 tbs. olive oil*
*1 cup hot water*     *1 tsp. sage*
*Salt and pepper to taste*

Have rabbit thoroughly cleaned. Wash in cold water. Place in deep pan. Cover with cold water; add 1 tablespoon of salt. Marinate 4 hours, then remove. Rinse with fresh water; dry with absorbent paper.

Sprinkle inside with sage, salt, and pepper. Insert 2 slices of bacon. Place 4 slices of bacon over rabbit. Place in baking pan. Pour in oil; arrange onions and carrots around rabbit. Roast in hot oven about 30 minutes or until brown on both sides. Baste occasionally. Lower flame. Add hot water; continue roasting about 30 minutes more or until tender. Baste occasionally.

Serve very hot with vegetables and salad. Serves 4 to 6.

## CONIGLIO ALLA CACCIATORA #1

### RABBIT HUNTER'S STYLE #1

*1 rabbit (3 or 4 lbs.)*          *1 tsp. chopped parsley*
*3 tbs. butter*                   *2 tbs. salt*
*2 tbs. olive oil*                *¾ cup dry sherry*
*1 stalk celery, chopped*         *1 tbs. tomato paste*
*1 chopped carrot*                *Salt and pepper to taste*
*1 medium onion, chopped*

Have rabbit cleaned and cut into serving pieces. Place in deep dish. Cover with cold water. Add 2 tablespoons of salt; marinate for 4 hours. Dry with absorbent paper.

Melt butter and olive oil in hot skillet. Brown rabbit on all sides (about 10 minutes). Lower flame; add all chopped vegetables, salt and pepper to taste. Cover. Simmer about 10 minutes. Blend tomato paste and sherry; add gradually, stirring frequently to prevent burning. Cover; simmer over low flame about 45 minutes or until rabbit is tender. If necessary, add a small quantity of water to make additional gravy.

Serve very hot with boiled rice. Serves 4 to 6.

## CONIGLIO ALLA CACCIATORA #2

### RABBIT HUNTER'S STYLE #2

*1 rabbit (4 or 5 lbs.)*          *1 clove garlic*
*1½ cups burgundy*                *2 cups canned tomatoes*
*4 tbs. olive oil*                *Pinch of rosemary*
*1 chopped onion*                 *Salt and pepper to taste*

Have rabbit cleaned and cut into small serving pieces. Place in bowl. Pour burgundy over it. Allow to marinate for 6 hours.

Heat olive oil in large saucepan. Add chopped onion; brown 3 minutes. Add rabbit, garlic, tomatoes, salt, and pepper. Cover; cook slowly 30 minutes. Gradually add the burgundy in which rabbit marinated. Add rosemary. Cook 20 minutes or until rabbit is tender.

Serve very hot. Serves 4 to 6.

# UMIDO DI CONIGLIO

## RABBIT STEW

*1 rabbit (3-4 lbs.)*                    *1 No. 2 can tomatoes*
*4 tbs. olive oil*                       *4 medium-sized potatoes*
*2 medium onions,*                       *1 cup water*
  *chopped*                              *Salt and pepper to taste*
              *⅛ tsp. crushed red pepper seeds*

Have rabbit cleaned and cut into serving pieces. Place
in enamel pot. Cover with water to which 2 tablespoons
of salt have been added. Let it stand for 2 hours, then
wash in cold running water and dry with absorbent paper.

Heat oil in pot. Sauté rabbit and onion for about 20
minutes. Season with salt and pepper; continue browning.
Add tomatoes. Cover tightly; cook slowly for about 20
minutes. Add quartered potatoes and 1 cup of water. Continue cooking ½ hour longer or until rabbit and potatoes
are tender.

Serves 4.

# CONIGLIO DOLCE E AGRO

## RABBIT SWEET AND SOUR

*1 rabbit (3 or 4 lbs.)*                 *1 clove garlic, chopped*
*2 tbs. tomato paste*                    *1 cup dry sauterne*
*2 ozs. olive oil*                       *2 tbs. raisins*
*1 tbs. chopped salt pork*               *2 tbs. pine nuts*
*1 tbs. chopped parsley*                 *¼ tsp. crushed red pep-*
*1 tsp. sugar*                             *per seeds*
*1 tbs. wine vinegar*                    *½ cup warm water*
              *Salt and pepper to taste*

Have rabbit cleaned and cut into small serving pieces.

Place olive oil and chopped salt pork in pot with parsley, garlic, and crushed pepper seeds. Add rabbit and
brown well for about 30 minutes. Add salt and very little
pepper, sugar, and vinegar; stir well. Pour ½ cup of
sauterne over it. Cover; simmer 10 minutes. Add tomato

paste blended in ½ cup of warm water. Lower flame; add nuts and raisins. Cover tightly; simmer about 20 minutes or until tender. Add remaining sauterne. Turn flame high; boil 1 minute.

Serve very hot. Serves 4 to 6.

# *Fowl*

## ANITRA AL COGNAC

### BRANDIED DUCK

| | |
|---|---|
| 1 duck (6 lbs.) | ½ lb. mushrooms |
| 2 large onions, chopped | ¼ cup olive oil |
| 2 tsp. chopped parsley | 3 jiggers cognac |
| 1 bay leaf | 1 clove garlic |
| Pinch of thyme | 1 pint claret |

Salt and pepper to taste

Have duck cleaned and cut into serving pieces. Sprinkle lightly with salt and pepper. Put in deep enamel dish. Add onions, parsley, bay leaf, thyme, garlic, cognac, and claret. Marinate for 4 hours.

Put oil in earthenware casserole; heat over high flame. Brown duck in oil for about 12 minutes. Then add liquid and sliced mushrooms. Cover; simmer over low flame for 1 hour or until duck is tender.

Serve hot. Enough for 4 to 6.

## FAGIANO O CONIGLIO SELVAGGIO

### PHEASANT OR WILD RABBIT

Use about 4 pounds of pheasant or wild rabbit and follow the same recipe and directions as for Venison Mario.

While roasting, add bay leaf to gravy for additional flavor.


## PERNICE AL FORNO

### ROASTED PARTRIDGE

1 partridge (about 4
   lbs.)
6 slices bacon

3 ozs. butter
½ tsp. sage
Salt and pepper to taste

Wash partridge thoroughly; wipe well with damp cloth. Rub inside and outside with butter. Sprinkle inside with sage. Arrange bacon strips over partridge. Place in roasting pan. Roast in hot oven 20 minutes or until golden brown. Baste occasionally. Add ½ cup of hot water to bottom of pan if dry. Lower flame; sprinkle with salt and pepper; roast 25 minutes longer or until tender. Continue basting. Remove from oven. Use pan gravy.

Serve very hot. Serves 4.


## PICCIONE SAUTÉ

### PIGEON SAUTÉ

4 plump pigeons
4 tbs. olive oil
1 tsp. sage
1 tsp. chopped parsley

½ cup hot water
⅛ lb. butter
1 lemon slice
4 slices bacon

Salt and pepper to taste

Have pigeons cleaned thoroughly. Brush with olive oil. Insert little butter and pinch of sage inside each pigeon. Sprinkle outside lightly with salt and pepper.

Brown bacon slightly in skillet over low flame. Remove. Brown pigeons about 5 minutes on each side. Lower flame; replace bacon. Add hot water, parsley, and lemon. Cover; simmer for 10 minutes or until tender.

Serve very hot. Serves 4.

## PICCIONI RIPIENI

### STUFFED PIGEONS

| | |
|---|---|
| *4 plump pigeons* | *¼ cup Romano cheese* |
| *1 cup bread crumbs* | *1 sliced lemon* |
| *¼ tsp. marjoram* | *2 tbs. butter* |
| *1 chopped onion* | *6 tbs. olive oil* |
| *1 tsp. chopped parsley* | *4 slices bacon* |
| *½ cup hot water* | *Salt and pepper to taste* |

Have pigeons thoroughly cleaned and washed. Cut off wing tips. Brush with olive oil; sprinkle with salt and pepper to taste.

Mix all ingredients except bacon; blend thoroughly. Stuff pigeons. Skewer them. Wrap slice of bacon around each. Pour balance of oil in baking dish. Place pigeons in it. Roast in medium oven about 20 minutes or until brown and tender. Baste occasionally. Add ½ cup of hot water. Roast 10 minutes more.

Serve hot with lemon slices and green salad. Serves 4.


## POLLO AL BURRO

### BUTTERED CHICKEN

| | |
|---|---|
| *1 roasting chicken (3½-* | *2 cloves garlic* |
| *4 lbs.)* | *¼ lb. butter* |
| *2 tbs. olive oil* | *3 sprigs parsley* |
| | *Salt and pepper to taste* |

Wash and dry chicken thoroughly. Rub inside with half of butter. Insert parsley, 1 clove of garlic. Sprinkle with salt and pepper. Sew or skewer opening.

Rub outside of chicken with salt and balance of butter. Put 1 clove of garlic, oil, and chicken in baking pan. Roast in moderate oven for about 1 hour or until golden brown and tender. Baste occasionally with pan juice.

Cut into serving pieces; serve very hot. Serves 4.

If you wish to serve whole pan-browned potatoes, peel 8 small ones. After chicken has roasted for about 30 minutes, add the potatoes; turn occasionally to brown. If pan is dry, add 1 tablespoon of oil and ½ cup of water. Potatoes will be done in about 30 minutes.

## POLLO ALLA CACCIATORA #1

### CHICKEN HUNTER'S STYLE #1

| | |
|---|---|
| *1 frying chicken (4 lbs.)* | *1 clove garlic, chopped* |
| *4 small onions* | *1 cup canned tomatoes* |
| *5 tbs. olive oil* | *1 cup sliced mushrooms* |
| *½ cup flour* | *1 large green pepper* |

*Salt and pepper to taste*

Cut chicken into serving pieces. Season with salt and pepper; roll lightly in flour. Heat oil in skillet and brown chicken on all sides about 10 minutes.

Stem, seed, and slice green pepper lengthwise. Mix with onions, garlic, and tomatoes; add mixture to chicken. Cover; simmer slowly for 40 minutes. Add mushrooms; simmer 15 minutes or until mushrooms and chicken are tender.

Serve very hot. Serves 4 to 6.

## POLLO ALLA CACCIATORA #2

### CHICKEN HUNTER'S STYLE #2

| | |
|---|---|
| *1 roasting chicken (4 lbs.)* | *1 medium onion, chopped* |
| *2 tbs. butter* | *1 tsp. chopped parsley* |
| *3 tbs. olive oil* | *1 tbs. tomato paste* |
| *1 stalk celery, chopped* | *¾ cup dry sherry* |
| *1 medium carrot, chopped* | *Salt and pepper to taste* |

Have chicken cleaned and cut into serving pieces.

Melt butter and olive oil in hot skillet. Brown chicken on each side about 5 minutes. Add all chopped vegetables, salt and pepper to taste. Simmer about 10 minutes or until vegetables are partially tender. Gradually add sherry into which tomato paste has been well blended. Cover.

Stir occasionally to prevent sticking. Simmer about 30 minutes or until chicken is tender. If these is insufficient gravy, add small quantity of water from time to time. Serve very hot. Serves 4 to 6.

## POLLO COLLA MARSALA

### CHICKEN WITH MARSALA

| | |
|---|---|
| *1 roasting chicken (4 lbs.)* | *¼ cup water* |
| *4 ozs. butter* | *½ cup marsala (heavy sweet sherry)* |
| *1 sliced onion* | *Salt and pepper to taste* |

Have chicken cleaned and cut into serving pieces. Sprinkle lightly with salt and pepper to taste. Melt butter in skillet. When very hot, add chicken. Brown on both sides about 5 minutes. Add onion; brown 2 minutes. Lower flame; add water; cover; simmer about 20 minutes or until tender. Add marsala; simmer for 10 minutes. If necessary, add small quantity of water.

Serve very hot. Serves 4 generous portions.

## POLLO CON FUNGHI

### CHICKEN WITH MUSHROOMS

| | |
|---|---|
| *1 broiler (3-4 lbs.)* | *6 tbs. olive oil* |
| *1 lb. fresh mushrooms* | *1 tbs. butter* |
| *2 cloves garlic* | *½ cup sherry* |
| *1 large onion, sliced* | *Salt and pepper to taste* |

Cut chicken into serving pieces; wash and dry thoroughly. Sprinkle lightly with salt and pepper to taste.

Heat butter in skillet; add garlic and 4 tablespoons of oil. Brown chicken on both sides about 10 minutes. Lower flame; cover; continue cooking for 25 minutes.

Sauté sliced onion in 2 tablespoons of olive oil in separate saucepan for 5 minutes. Add cleaned, sliced mushrooms and 2 tablespoons of water. Simmer 15 minutes; add to chicken. Cover. Simmer chicken and mushrooms

15 minutes longer. Pour in ½ cup sherry; boil up quickly
for 1 minute.

Serve very hot. Serves 4.


## POLLO CON ROSAMARINA

### CHICKEN WITH ROSEMARY

| | |
|---|---|
| *1 broiler (3-4 lbs.)* | *1 tsp. rosemary* |
| *3 tbs. olive oil* | *2 cloves garlic* |
| *1 tbs. butter* | *¼ cup water* |

*Salt and pepper to taste*

Have chicken cleaned and cut into serving pieces. Wash
and dry thoroughly. Sprinkle lightly with salt and pepper
to taste.

Melt butter in skillet. Add oil and garlic; heat. Brown
chicken on both sides about 10 minutes. Sprinkle with
rosemary. Gradually add a little water; cover; simmer
over low flame about 25 minutes or until tender. Gradually add more water, if necessary, to prevent burning.

Serve very hot. Serves 4.


## POLLO IMBOTTITO

### STUFFED CHICKEN

| | |
|---|---|
| *1 roasting chicken* | *1 tbs. olive oil* |
| *(4-5 lbs.)* | *¼ lb. butter* |

*Salt and pepper to taste*

*Stuffing:*

| | |
|---|---|
| *½ cup boiled rice* | *¼ tsp. marjoram* |
| *½ cup bread crumbs* | *1 clove garlic, chopped* |
| *1 egg* | *2 tsp. chopped parsley* |
| *2 strips chopped pro-* | *3 tbs. grated Romano* |
| *sciutto (Italian ham)* | *cheese* |
| *2 tbs. olive oil* | *Salt and pepper to taste* |

Wash and dry chicken thoroughly. Rub outside with
half of butter and 1 tablespoon of olive oil. Salt and pepper to taste.

Mix all stuffing ingredients thoroughly. If dry, add 1 tablespoon of milk. Stuff chicken; sew or skewer together to prevent stuffing from falling out. Place chicken and balance of butter in roasting pan. Brown on both sides in very hot oven. If pan is too dry, add ¼ cup of hot water to keep moist. After 30 minutes, lower flame; continue roasting in moderate oven 1 hour longer or until chicken is tender. Baste occasionally.

Serves 6.

## POLLO IN UMIDO

### CHICKEN STEW

| | |
|---|---|
| 1 roasting chicken (4 lbs.) | Pinch of marjoram |
| 2 sliced onions | 2 cups hot water |
| 1 cup canned tomatoes | 1 cup boiled fresh peas |
| 4 tbs. olive oil | 1 tbs. chopped parsley |
| | 1 cup diced potatoes |

Salt and pepper to taste

Have chicken cleaned and cut into serving pieces. Wash and dry thoroughly.

Brown chicken slightly in hot oil for about 10 minutes. Sprinkle lightly with salt and pepper. Add onion; simmer for 5 minutes. Then add parsley, marjoram, tomatoes and 1 cup of hot water. Cover; simmer about 30 minutes. Add potatoes and peas. Continue cooking for ½ hour or until chicken and potatoes are tender. If stew has absorbed too much liquid, gradually add a little hot water to make sufficient gravy.

Serves 4 to 6.

## POLLO OREGANATO

### CHICKEN ORÉGANO

| | |
|---|---|
| 1 broiler (about 4 lbs.) | ⅓ cup olive oil |
| 1 tsp. chopped parsley | ¼ cup lemon juice |
| 2 tsp. orégano | 1 clove garlic, chopped |

Salt and pepper to taste

Have broiler cleaned and quartered. Sprinkle lightly with salt and pepper.

Mix olive oil, orégano, lemon juice, garlic, and parsley thoroughly. Brush chicken generously with this mixture. Place on broiler rack about 6 inches beneath high flame. Broil about 20 minutes on each side or until brown and tender. Brush occasionally with liquid to prevent dryness. When done, pour balance of liquid over chicken and serve very hot.

Serves 4.

## QUAGLIA ALLA GRIGLIA

### BROILED QUAIL

*6 quail*                          *6 tsp. butter*
*6 slices bacon*                   *Salt and pepper to taste*

Have quail cleaned thoroughly. Wash. Dry with damp cloth. Sprinkle inside with salt and pepper; place 1 teaspoon of butter in each bird. Wrap slice of bacon around each.

Place quail on broiler rack about 6 inches below medium flame. Broil about 10 minutes on each side or until golden brown and tender.

Serve very hot on toast. Serves 6.

# CHAPTER TWELVE

# Desserts

## CAFFE ESPRESSO

### BLACK COFFEE

| | |
|---|---|
| *6 tbs. Italian-roasted* | *Peel of 1 lemon* |
| *coffee* | *or* |
| *6 cups water* | *12 tsp. cognac* |

*1 Caffettiera (Italian coffee maker)*

Use coffee which has been roasted very black in the Italian manner. Have it pulverized. In American stores it is identified as "French-roasted" but is called Italian-roasted in all Italian stores. In some sections of the country pulverized Italian coffee may be purchased in cans.

An Italian coffee maker called a "Caffettiera" may be purchased in any Italian store which carries pottery and hardware.

The "Caffettiera" has two sections: the lower part holds a strainer-top container for the coffee; the upper has an inverted spout.

Remove top part; lift out strainer-top container from the lower part; fill with coffee. Place water in bottom section. Replace container. Cover with top section.

Place over high flame. When steam escapes from tiny opening in lower section, the water is boiling. Grasp handles firmly; remove from fire and reverse the entire "Caffettiera" quickly. The boiling water drips through the coffee in a few moments and the Caffe Espresso is ready to serve.

To keep very hot, allow to stand over low flame. Never reheat.

SECTIONS OF COFFEE-MAKER          BOILING POSITION

POSITION FOR DRIPPING            SERVING POSITION

May be served in 4-ounce glasses with a twist of lemon peel, or in a demitasse with cognac. Serves 12.

## AMARETTI

### MACAROONS

½ lb. sugar
¼ lb. shelled blanched
  almonds

¼ tsp. almond extract
2 egg whites

Chop and pulverize almonds; mix thoroughly with half of sugar and extract.

Beat eggwhites until very stiff. Add balance of sugar; beat again. Add almond mixture; mix thoroughly. Shape into balls or cookies about 2 inches in diameter. Place on greased cookie pan about 1 inch apart. Bake in moderate oven about 5 minutes or until light brown.

Makes about 1 dozen, depending upon size desired.

## BISCOTTI AL'ANICI

### AUNT LENA'S ANISE SLICES

| | |
|---|---|
| 6 eggs | ½ lb. butter or shorten- |
| 1 lb. flour | ing |
| 6 drops anise oil (pur- | ½ cup sugar |
| chased at drugstore) | 1 tsp. baking powder |

½ teaspoon salt

Beat 5 eggs with salt; add sugar; blend thoroughly.

Sift flour and baking powder; add to eggs and sugar mixture. Add anise oil (which may be purchased at a drugstore), softened butter or shortening; mix well. Knead until dough is smooth and manageable. Then roll dough into oblong loaf 5 inches broad and about ¾ inch thick. Brush with 1 beaten egg; sprinkle with sugar; cut into 1-inch slices.

Place slices in greased baking pan; bake for 15 minutes in moderate oven, or until light brown.

Enough for 2½ dozen slices. An unusual flavor!

## BISCOTTI DI ZIA LENA

### AUNT LENA'S COOKIES

| | |
|---|---|
| 3 cups flour | ½ cup shortening |
| 2 tps. baking powder | ½ cup sugar |
| 2 eggs | ¼ cup milk |
| ½ cup chopped walnuts | ½ tsp. cinnamon |

Pinch of salt

Mix all dry ingredients except nuts; blend shortening with hands; beat eggs and add to mixture. Add milk gradually and form into a ball. Knead and mold dough until smooth. Roll small pieces into 3-inch oblong shapes. Sprinkle tops with chopped nuts. Bake in moderate oven about 15 minutes or until golden brown.

Makes about 3 dozen, depending upon size desired.

## CASSATA ALLA SICILIANA

### CREAM TART SICILIAN

*1 spongecake (10-12 in. in diameter)*
*½ cup sugar*
*¼ lb. glazed mixed fruit*
*1½ lbs. ricotta (Italian cottage cheese)*
*2 squares bitter chocolate, chopped*
*2 tsp. almond extract*

Strain ricotta through wire sieve to refine. Add sugar; mix thoroughly. Add chocolate and almond extract; blend until custard-like consistency is obtained. Set aside in cold place until ready to use.

Cut plain spongecake in 3 layers. Put bottom layer in large round dish. Spread about ½ inch thick with filling. Top this with another layer of cake, then another ½ inch of the filling. Top layer should be spongecake. Set in refrigerator until this frosting is ready:

*1 egg white*
*1 tsp. almond extract*
*1½ cups sifted confectioners' sugar*
*½ tsp. lemon juice*

Gradually mix 1 cup of sugar with egg white; beat with spoon until smooth. Add flavoring and lemon juice; blend with more sugar (about ½ cup) until thick enough to spread.

Cover sides and top of Cassata evenly. Place cherry in center. Distribute glazed fruit on top to form an attractive design. Sprinkle with nuts and citron if desired.

Serves 10 to 12.

## CASSATELLE ALLA SICILIANA

### SICILIAN CREAM TARTLETS

*Dough:*

| | |
|---|---|
| 1 lb. flour | 2 tbs. claret |
| 1 egg | 3 tbs. shortening |
| 4 tbs. tepid water | 1 tsp. vanilla |
| 2 tbs. sugar | 2 tsp. baking powder |

*Pinch of salt*

Dissolve sugar in tepid water. Mix all other ingredients except claret. Add water slowly. Knead well. While dough is stiff, gradually add wine. Continue kneading until dough can be rolled out easily. Place in bowl. Set aside in cool place for 30 minutes.

In the meantime, prepare this cream filling:

| | |
|---|---|
| 1 lb. ricotta (Italian cottage cheese) | 1 tsp. almond flavor |
| 1 square bitter chocolate, chopped | 4 tbs. sugar |
| | 2 tbs. grated orange rind |
| 1 tbs. chopped citron | 1 tsp. grated lemon rind |
| | 1 pt. peanut oil |

Blend all ingredients, except peanut oil, thoroughly until a custard-like consistency is obtained. If too dry, add a little milk and continue blending. Place in bowl. Set in refrigerator until used.

Cut dough into 3 sections. Roll out on lightly floured board until very thin. Cut dough into disks about 3 inches in diameter. Fry in very deep hot oil 1 minute or until golden brown on both sides. Drain on brown paper. Set aside to cool.

When disks are cold, put one in palm of hand and spread with a tablespoon of cream filling; top with another disk. This forms the tartlet. Repeat until all are used. Sprinkle with powdered sugar.

Makes about 2 dozen. A real treat for the holidays.

# FARFALLETTE DOLCI

## SWEET BOWKNOTS

6 eggs
3 tbs. granulated sugar
3 cups flour
½ tsp. orange flavor

½ cup powdered sugar
¼ tsp. salt
2 tbs. butter
1 tsp. almond flavor

· 3 cups peanut oil

Beat eggs lightly; add granulated sugar, salt, and flavoring; blend thoroughly.

Place flour on board; cut in butter; add egg mixture. Knead until smooth ball is obtained. If dough is too soft, gradually add a little flour to make firm but not hard. Set aside for 30 minutes.

Then cut dough in 4 sections. Roll on· well-floured board until wafer-thin. Cut with pastry cutter into strips 6 inches long by ¾ inch wide. Tie in individual bowknots. Fry bows about 3 minutes or until light brown in deep hot peanut oil. Drain on absorbent paper; cool; sprinkle with powdered sugar.

Makes about 6 to 7 dozen bowknots.

# LA CREMA

## DE LUXE CREAM CAKE

4 eggs
4 tbs. sugar
4 cups milk
4 tbs. cornstarch
Rind of one lemon, cut
  in one piece

2 lbs. plain poundcake
1 oz. bittersweet chocolate, chopped
1 tsp. almond extract
1 maraschino cherry
2 tbs. diced citron

Blend cornstarch in ½ cup milk. Combine with rest of milk, eggs, sugar, and lemon rind. Blend thoroughly in saucepan.

Cook over slow fire about 10 minutes; stir constantly until it comes to a boil. Remove from fire immediately; take out lemon rind; add almond extract. Cool.

Slice poundcake in ¼-in thick slices. Arrange 1 layer of cake on bottom of 10-inch pie plate; pour some of mixture (about ½ inch thick) over this. Alternate until all cake and mixture is used. The top layer should be cream. Place in refrigerator 4 to 5 hours or until ready to serve. Then sprinkle chopped chocolate and citron over top with a cherry in center for color.

Serves 10 to 12.

## PALLOTTOLE D'ARANCI

### ORANGE BALLS

| | |
|---|---|
| ½ lb. fresh orange peels | ½ lb. sugar |
| ¼ lb. chopped mixed nuts | 1 tsp. vanilla |

Use about six large California oranges. Peel thickly with sharp knife. Soak peels in cold water for 24 hours. Drain. Weigh peels. Place in saucepan; cover with cold water; bring to a boil. Cook about 10 minutes or until soft; drain.

Chop orange peels fine; mix with sugar; cook slowly over low flame about 10 minutes or until a small quantity dropped into cold water forms a soft ball. Add vanilla; blend thoroughly. Remove from fire; cool; shape into small balls about size of small walnut. Roll in sugar; dip in finely chopped nuts. Something different!

## PANE DI SPAGNA

### SPONGE CAKE

| | |
|---|---|
| 8 egg yolks | 1⅓ cups flour |
| 8 egg whites | 1¼ cups sugar |
| 2 tsp. grated lemon rind | 1½ tbs. water |
| 2 tsp. almond extract | ¼ tsp. salt |

Use large mixing bowl. Sift ½ cup of sugar with flour several times to blend well. Place egg yolks, water, and grated lemon rind in bowl. Beat lightly; add almond extract. Gradually sift flour very lightly over beaten egg yolks. Fold in gently.

Place egg whites in another mixing bowl and beat until foamy. Add salt and balance of sugar; beat until stiff. Gently fold the stiff egg whites into flour mixture. Pour into 10- or 12-inch ungreased cake pan. Bake in moderate oven 45 minutes, or until cake separates from sides of pan. Be careful not to jar cake while baking, as it may become heavy.

When cake is done, invert pan on wire rack for about 1 hour or until cold. Remove from pan.

## PERE RIPIENE ALLA MILANESE

### STUFFED PEARS MILANESE

| | |
|---|---|
| 6 large firm pears | 1/4 lb. shelled toasted |
| 3 ozs. powdered sugar | almonds |
| 4 maraschino cherries | 1/4 tsp. almond extract |
| 1/2 cup dry sherry | |

Wash pears. Cut in half lengthwise; scoop out cores. Chop cherries very fine. Grind almonds until almost mealy; add extract. Blend very thoroughly all ingredients except sherry.

Fill pear halves with this mixture. Place in baking dish. Pour sherry over pears; bake in medium oven about 15 minutes, or until pears are done but not too soft.

Serve either very hot or cooled, as preferred. Serves 6 to 8.

## PESCA CON VINO ROSSO

### PEACH WITH BURGUNDY

| | |
|---|---|
| 1 large ripe peach | 2 ozs. burgundy |
| | (chilled) |

Peel one large ripe peach; slice lengthwise. Place in large sherbet glass; pour 2 ounces of burgundy over peach. Serve immediately. Serves 1.

## PESCHE IMBOTTITE ALLA MANDORLA

### PEACHES STUFFED WITH ALMONDS

6 large firm fresh peaches                2 ozs. shelled toasted
  or                                        almonds
12 halves canned peaches                  3 ozs. powdered sugar
1 tbs. chopped glazed                     ½ cup dry sherry
  orange peel or citron

Peel, pit, and halve fresh peaches. Chop and pulverize almonds until mealy; add half the sugar; mix thoroughly. Add citron or orange peel; blend. Then fill peach halves. Place in baking pan. Sprinkle with balance of sugar; pour in sherry. Bake in moderate oven 10 minutes.
Serve warm. Serves 6.

## PASTICCIO

### FLAKY PIE CRUST

2½ cups flour                    1 tsp. almond extract
⅓ cup ice water                  ¾ tsp. salt
          1 cup butter or shortening

Sift together flour and salt. Gently blend in shortening; add flavoring; gradually add sufficient water to hold ingredients together. Gently form a smooth ball. Cut in half.
Roll out dough in circular piece about ⅛ inch thick on lightly floured board.
Sufficient for a 2-crust 8- or 9-inch pie.

## PIGNOLATA-STRUFOLI

### PINE-NUT CLUSTERS

2 eggs                           ½ cup honey
2 cups flour                     2 tbs. pine nuts
2 cups peanut oil                1 tbs. colored candied
¼ tsp. salt                        confetti
          ½ cup sugar

Place 1 cup of flour on board; break in eggs; add salt; knead together gently. Gradually add enough flour to make medium-soft, easily molded dough. Texture becomes soft with kneading. When very smooth, cut in half.

Roll out dough in circular piece about ¼ inch thick on lightly floured board. Cut into strips about ¼ inch wide. Mold each strip gently to resemble a small rope about 10 inches long (on lightly floured board). Cut into tiny pieces about ¼ inch. Each bit of dough resembles a grape or small marble. Distribute on lightly floured board to prevent sticking.

Heat oil in deep saucepan. When very hot, gradually add small pieces (about 6 tablespoons at a time), stirring constantly with wooden spoon. Brown lightly for 1 or 2 minutes; remove with perforated spoon. Drain on absorbent paper.

Blend sugar and honey in large deep skillet; stir constantly. Heat about 5 minutes over low flame. When very smooth, add all browned pieces, stirring constantly with wooden spoon. When covered with honey mixture, remove quickly; place on 2 large platters. Mold with spoon into desired forms (as bunches of grapes or small clusters). Top each form with pine nuts; sprinkle with colored confetti. Allow to cool.

Serve by breaking off individual pieces with cake fork. Pignolata-Strufoli keeps fresh for 2 weeks when placed in cakebox. Serves 8 to 10.

## SFINGE DI SAN GIUSEPPE

### ST. JOSEPH'S CREAM PUFFS

| | |
|---|---|
| ¼ lb. butter | 4 eggs |
| ¼ tsp. salt | 1 tbs. sugar |
| 1 cup flour | 1 tbs. grated lemon rind |
| 1 cup water | 1 tsp. grated orange rind |
| 18 maraschino cherries | ½ cup glazed orange peel |

Place water and butter in saucepan; bring to a boil. Add flour and salt; keep stirring until mixture leaves sides of pan or forms a ball in the center. Remove from stove and cool. Add eggs one at a time, beating each in thoroughly.

Add sugar, orange peel, and lemon rind; mix well. Drop by tablespoon on cooky pan, placing the puffs about 3 inches apart, or put in muffin tins.

Heat oven to 400 degrees and bake 10 minutes. Then reduce temperature to 350 and bake about ½ hour or until light brown. Remove from oven. Open puffs immediately to allow steam to escape. (Puffs should be opened through center top.) Cool. Fill with Ricotta Filling; top with a cherry and two thin slices of glazed orange peel. (A plain custard filling may be substituted if desired.)

*Ricotta Filling:*

| | |
|---|---|
| *1 lb. ricotta (Italian cottage cheese)* | *1 tbs. grated orange rind* |
| | *Sugar to taste* |
| *2 tbs. grated chocolate* | *3 tbs. milk* |

*2 tsp. almond extract*

Blend all ingredients thoroughly. Use milk sparingly, and only if needed to make smooth custard-like mixture. Put in refrigerator until used.

, Recipe makes approximately 18 cream puffs.


## SAVOIARDI

### LADY FINGERS

| | |
|---|---|
| *2 cups sifted flour* | *2 tsp. baking powder* |
| *1 cup sugar* | *1 tbs. almond extract* |
| *4 eggs* | *Pinch of salt* |

Beat sugar and eggs until thoroughly blended and cream-colored. Mix flour, salt, and baking powder; sift slowly into egg mixture. Keep beating until smooth, creamy consistency is obtained. (Use of an electric mixer is advisable since it reduces work and will produce a smoother batter.)

Butter cooky pans generously and sprinkle with a little flour. Drop batter by spoonfuls, shaping it about 3 inches long and 1 inch wide. Place about 1½ inches apart, as they spread when baking. Bake in medium oven about 10 minutes or until light brown.

Enough for 3 dozen, depending upon size and shape.

# SPUMONI

## ITALIAN ICE CREAM

*Mixture # 1  Outside Custard:*

1 qt. milk  
4 tbs. cornstarch  
1¼ cups sugar

2 tbs. chopped almonds  
5 egg yolks  
⅛ tsp. salt

*Mixture # 2  Cream Filling:*

½ pt. heavy cream  
½ cup sugar  
6 maraschino cherries

2 tbs. candied orange  
peel

Prepare Mixture #1 as follows:

Blend cornstarch in ½ cup of milk. Combine with balance of milk, egg yolks, and sugar. Blend thoroughly in deep saucepan.

Cook very slowly over hot water; stir constantly, about 10 minutes or until mixture thickens and comes to a boil. Remove from fire immediately. Stir in chopped almonds. Cool.

Pour into freezing tray of refrigerator. When firm but not hard, remove from tray.

While Mixture #1 is freezing, prepare Mixture #2 as follows:

Pour cream in deep chilled mixing bowl; whip until firm. Add sugar; whip until very thick. Chop maraschino cherries and orange peel very fine; blend into whipped cream. Place bowl in refrigerator to keep cold and stiff while preparing molds.

Spumoni molds are always made to order. If unable to purchase them, use 10 to 12 individual aluminum, covered jello molds.

Chill molds before using.

Remove Mixture #1 (outside custard) from freezing tray. Line individual molds with 1-inch thickness of this partially frozen custard. Leave hollow in center of mold. Fill hollow with Mixture #2 (cream filling). Cover with Mixture #1. Cover molds. If molds are without covers, protect spumoni by covering with 2 thicknesses of heavy waxed paper.

Place individual molds in freezing compartment of refrigerator at degree set for freezing.

Makes enough spumoni to serve 10 to 12.

## TORTA DI PISTACCHIO

### PISTACHIO PIE

*Pastry:*

| | |
|---|---|
| *2 cups flour* | *¼ lb. butter* |
| *1 egg* | *½ cup sugar* |
| *¼ tsp. salt* | *2 tbs. sherry* |

Sift together flour, sugar, and salt. Beat egg lightly. Blend all ingredients with butter in deep bowl. Gradually add enough sherry to form firm pastry. Roll in circular piece about ⅛ inch thick to fit 9- or 10-inch pie plate. Butter plate before placing pastry in it. For an even fluted standing rim, pinch edges of pastry. Cut balance of pastry in strips ½ inch wide to use as a crisscross (lattice) top.

*Pistachio Filling:*

| | |
|---|---|
| *1 pt. sweet milk* | *¾ cup whole-wheat flour* |
| *2 eggs* | *¼ tsp. nutmeg* |
| *4 ozs. pistachio nuts* | *1 tbs. powdered sugar* |
| *2 ozs. granulated sugar* | *Pinch of salt* |

Chop nuts medium-fine. Place flour in deep saucepan. Gradually blend in milk until mixture is very smooth. Add granulated sugar, beaten eggs, salt, and nutmeg. Blend thoroughly. Place over medium flame; stir constantly to prevent lumping and sticking; bring to a boil. Lower flame; cook for 10 minutes; continue stirring. Gradually add nuts. Continue stirring vigorously until all is a well-blended, very smooth custard. Remove from fire; cool. Pour filling into prepared pastry; place lattice strips over top. Pinch edges lightly. Bake in moderately hot oven for 45 minutes or until mixture is firm but not dry and pastry is golden brown. Remove from oven; cool. Sprinkle with powdered sugar just before serving.

Serves 10.

## ZABAGLIONE

### MARSALA CUSTARD

6 egg yolks                          6 level tsp. sugar
6 half eggshells full of marsala (heavy sweet sherry)

Break egg yolks into top part of large double boiler. Add sugar. Beat with egg beater until light lemon color and thoroughly blended. Add marsala. Beat thoroughly again.

Place boiling water in lower part of double boiler. Cook egg-yolk mixture (over boiling water) about 5 minutes or until it begins to thicken. While cooking be sure to beat constantly. Do not allow to boil. Remove from fire immediately upon first sign of bubble. Cool. Place in refrigerator.

Serve cold in sherbet or parfait glasses. Serves 6.

## TORTA DI RICOTTA

### ITALIAN CHEESE PIE

Pastry:

2 cups flour                          2/3 cup butter or shortening
2 tbs. dry sherry                     1/2 tsp. salt

Sift together flour and salt. Cut in butter or shortening; gradually add sherry. If necessary, add a little water to hold mixture firmly. Do not knead too much. Roll in circular piece about 1/8 inch thick to fit 9- or 10-inch pie plate. Butter plate before placing pastry in it. Cut balance of pastry in strips ½ inch wide to use as crisscross (lattice) top.

*Filling:* ·

| | |
|---|---|
| 1½ lbs. ricotta (Italian cottage cheese) | 1 tsp. vanilla flavoring |
| | 4 eggs |
| ¼ lb. toasted almonds | ⅓ cup granulated sugar |
| 1 tbs. chopped citron | 2 tbs. powdered sugar |

Chop almonds fine; add ricotta and mix thoroughly. Beat eggs and granulated sugar well; add vanilla. Add to ricotta; stir until well blended and smooth.

Pour ricotta filling into prepared pastry; place lattice strips over top. Pinch edges lightly. Bake in moderately hot oven 45 minutes or until mixture is firm but not dry and pastry is golden brown. Remove from oven; cool. Sprinkle with powdered sugar just before serving.

Serves 10.

## ZUPPA INGLESE #1

(Literally means "soup" but is an Italian rum cake covered with custard)

| | |
|---|---|
| 1 qt. milk | 6 tbs. orange marmalade |
| 6 egg yolks | 1 large spongecake |
| 8 tbs. sugar | (about 12 in.) |
| 8 tbs. flour | Pinch of salt |
| 1 grated lemon rind | 2 ozs. finely chopped |
| 12 tbs. sweet vermouth | toasted almonds |
| 12 tbs. sweet rum | |

*Plain Custard:*

Beat egg yolks thoroughly. Blend well in saucepan the milk, eggs, sugar, flour, and salt. Strain through fine sieve to insure very smooth mixture. Grate lemon rind; add this to mixture. Cook over low flame for about 10 minutes or until thick and it *starts* to boil. Do not boil. Remove from fire. Cool. If chocolate flavor is desired, melt two cubes of bitter chocolate in hot custard. Stir well.

*Spongecake:*

| | |
|---|---|
| *8 egg yolks* | *1¼ cup sugar* |
| *8 egg whites* | *2 tbs. water* |
| *1⅓ cups flour* | *1½ tsp. almond extract* |
| *2 tsp. grated lemon rind* | *¼ tsp. salt* |

Use large mixing bowl. Sift ½ cup of sugar with flour several times to blend well. Place egg yolks, water, and grated lemon rind in mixing bowl. Beat lightly. Add almond extract. Gradually sift flour very lightly over beaten egg yolks. Fold in gently. Place egg whites in another bowl and beat until foamy. Add salt and balance of sugar; beat until stiff. Gently fold in the stiff egg whites into flour mixture. Pour into 10- or 12-inch ungreased cake pan. Bake in moderate oven 45 minutes, or until cake separates from sides of pan. Be careful not to jar cake while baking, as it may become heavy.

When cake is done, invert pan on wire rack for about 1 hour or until cold. Remove from pan.

Slice spongecake into 3 layers; pour 6 tablespoons of vermouth over each of 2 layers. Spread with thin layer of orange marmalade, then layer of custard. Place third layer over this; pour rum over all. Cover top and sides of cake evenly with thick layer of custard. Sprinkle with finely chopped almonds.

Serves 12 to 14.

## ZUPPA INGLESE #2

### ITALIAN RUM CAKE

| | |
|---|---|
| *8 egg yolks* | *1 spongecake (10-12 in. in diameter)* |
| *8 half eggshells full of marsala (heavy sweet sherry)* | *1 cup sweet rum* |
| *8 level tsp. sugar* | *2 tbs. sugar* |
| | *½ pt. whipping cream* |
| | *½ cup chopped glazed fruit* |

*Zabaglione* (Marsala Custard): Break egg yolks into

top part of large double boiler. Add sugar. Beat with egg beater until light lemon color and thoroughly blended. Add marsala; beat thoroughly again.

Place boiling water in lower part of double boiler. Cook egg-yolk mixture (over boiling water) about 5 minutes or until it begins to thicken. While cooking, be sure to beat constantly. Do not allow to boil. Remove from fire immediately upon first sign of bubble. Set aside to cool.

Slice spongecake into three layers. Place one layer on cake plate; pour ⅓ cup of rum over it. Cover with ⅓ of Zabaglione. Place second layer of cake over this; alternate with rum and Zabaglione. Place in refrigerator. When ready to serve, pour cream in mixing bowl; add 2 tablespoons of sugar; whip until stiff. Spread over top and sides of cake just before serving. Sprinkle with chopped glazed fruit.

Serves 12 to 14.

# CHAPTER THIRTEEN

# Luncheon Delicacies

## Eggs

### FRITTATA DI CARNE E VEGETALI

#### VEGETABLE-MEAT OMELET

6 eggs
1 sliced onion
6 tbs. olive oil
2 cups cooked meat and vegetables

4 tbs. grated Romano
cheese
Salt and pepper to taste

Use any leftover meat and vegetables; chop fine. Heat 2 tablespoons of oil in large skillet. Brown onion about 3 minutes or until soft. Add meat and vegetables; mix well. Heat for 7 minutes; stir constantly. Transfer to mixing bowl. Beat eggs thoroughly in separate bowl; fold into omelet mixture; blend well.

Place balance of olive oil in frying pan. Heat. Fry omelet mixture about 5 minutes or until light brown on underside. Turn out carefully on a plate. If necessary, add more oil to frying pan. Slide omelet back into pan; brown other side.

Serve immediately. Serves 6 to 8.

### FRITTATA DI BROCCOLI

#### BROCCOLI OMELET

1 small bunch broccoli
4 eggs
4 tbs. olive oil

1 clove garlic, chopped
3 tbs. grated Parmesan
cheese
Salt and pepper to taste

139

Let broccoli stand in cold water 15 or 20 minutes. When crisp, peel; split stalks. Place in rapidly boiling salted water; cook about 15 minutes or until tender. Drain; cut crosswise in 1-inch pieces.

Beat eggs thoroughly in a large bowl; add salt, pepper, garlic, cheese, and broccoli; mix well.

Heat oil in large skillet; pour in mixture. Cook over low flame about 5 minutes or until omelet is fluffy and browned on under side. Turn carefully by using spatula. If necessary, place more oil in skillet. Brown on other side. Serve immediately. Serves 4 to 6.

## UOVA ALLA CACCIATORA

### EGGS HUNTER'S STYLE

| | |
|---|---|
| *4 eggs* | *¼ cup dry sauterne* |
| *4 chicken livers* | *1 tbs. tomato paste* |
| *3 tbs. olive oil* | *1 tbs. chopped onion* |
| *4 tbs. warm water* | *Salt and pepper to taste* |

Cut livers in half; season with salt and pepper. Heat oil in frying pan; sauté livers and onion for 5 minutes over low flame.

Blend tomato paste and warm water in a cup. Add to livers; simmer for 5 minutes. Add sauterne; cook for 3 minutes. Add eggs one at a time, being careful not to break yolks. Cover pan and cook 3 minutes or until whites are firm.

Serve very hot on toast. Serves 4.

## FRITTATA DI CIPOLLA

### ONION OMELET

| | |
|---|---|
| *4 eggs* | *1 large sweet onion* |
| *6 tbs. olive oil or butter* | *Salt and pepper to taste* |

Break eggs into deep bowl; add salt and pepper to

taste; beat lightly. Slice onion wafer-thin. Heat half oil or butter in skillet. Brown onion slightly for about 5 minutes. Remove; place in bowl. Add eggs; beat well. Heat balance of oil in skillet; cook eggs over low flame 3 to 5 minutes or until omelet is light and fluffy and browned on under side. Using spatula, turn over carefully. Brown lightly.

Serve immediately. Serves 4.

## UOVA FIORENTINA

### EGGS FLORENTINE

| | |
|---|---|
| *4 eggs* | *1½ lbs. fresh spinach* |
| *3 tbs. olive oil* | *Salt and pepper to taste* |

*4 tbs. grated Pecorino cheese*

Clean, wash, and drain spinach carefully. Put oil in saucepan; when hot, add spinach. Cover well; cook 10 to 12 minutes or until tender. Add salt and pepper to taste.

Arrange spinach in four individual ramekins. Break an egg over each; sprinkle 1 tablespoon of grated Pecorino cheese over top. Bake in moderate oven about 3 minutes or until egg white is firm but yolk is still soft.

Serves 4.

## UOVA CON OLIVE E PROVOLONE

### EGGS WITH OLIVES AND PROVOLONE

| | |
|---|---|
| *4 eggs* | *2 ozs. Provolone cheese* |
| *3 tbs. olive oil* | *Salt and pepper to taste* |

*12 large ripe Italian olives*

Pit olives; cut in half. Beat eggs thoroughly. Cut cheese into ½-inch pieces. Heat oil in frying pan or skillet. Add olives; sauté for 2 minutes. Add cheese; stir constantly for 1 minute over medium flame. Fold in beaten eggs, pinch of pepper. (Use salt very sparingly since olives and cheese are salty.) Stir until eggs are as firm as desired. Serve very hot. Serves 2.

## UOVA CON PEPERONI

### EGGS WITH PEPPERS

5 eggs
4 large firm green
  peppers

5 tbs. olive oil
1 clove garlic
Salt and pepper to taste

Clean, seed, and slice peppers lengthwise in 1-inch strips. Beat eggs thoroughly. Heat oil in large frying pan. When hot, add garlic and sliced peppers. Fry until slightly brown, about 5 minutes. Lower flame; cover pan; sauté slowly for 15 minutes or until peppers are soft. Fold in beaten eggs. Stir gently until eggs are of consistency desired. Remove from fire; serve immediately.
Serves 4.

## UOVA CON SALSA DI POMODORO

### EGGS WITH TOMATO SAUCE

6 eggs
4 tbs. olive oil
1 clove garlic, chopped
1 No. 2 can tomatoes

1 tbs. chopped parsley
Pinch of crushed red
  pepper seeds
1 small onion, sliced

Salt to taste

Heat olive oil in large shallow saucepan. Cook onion and garlic about 2 minutes or until soft. Add tomatoes, parsley, crushed pepper seeds, and salt to taste. Simmer over low flame about 25 minutes. Drop eggs in sauce one at a time, without breaking yolks. Cook slowly for 3 minutes or until egg whites are firm.
Serve hot. Serves 6.

# Rice

## ARANCINI DI RICOTTA

### STUFFED RICE CROQUETTES

¾ lb. rice
1 lb. ricotta (Italian
    cottage cheese)
2 eggs, well beaten

1 cup toasted bread
    crumbs
½ cup olive or peanut oil
Salt to taste

Cook rice in 3 quarts of rapidly boiling salted water about 25 minutes or until done. Drain and cool, spread 1 tablespoon of rice on palm of hand; place 1 tablespoon of ricotta over rice; sprinkle with salt; top with more rice; shape into round or oblong croquettes. Continue until all rice and ricotta are used. Dip croquettes in well-beaten egg; roll in bread crumbs. Fry in very hot olive or peanut oil about 3 minutes or until golden brown on all sides.

Serve hot as side dish with meat or fowl. May be served also as a dessert. Simply roll in powdered sugar and serve hot or cold.

Serves 6 to 8.

## CROCHE DI SPINACI

### RICE-SPINACH CROQUETTES

1 cup cooked rice
3 cups cooked spinach
3 eggs, slightly beaten
½ tsp. salt

6 tbs. olive oil
2 ozs. grated Pecorino
    cheese
⅛ tsp. pepper

Mix all ingredients, except oil, thoroughly until well blended. Heat oil in skillet. Drop heaping tablespoons of mixture into hot oil; fry about 3 minutes or until each side is golden brown. Serve very hot as a side dish, or as a main dish with vegetables.

Serves 4.

## CROCHE DI RISO

### RICE CROQUETTES

| | |
|---|---|
| ½ lb. rice | 2 tbs. chopped parsley |
| 2 eggs | 1 cup toasted bread |
| 4 ozs. grated Parmesan | crumbs |
| cheese | 2 cups peanut oil |

Salt and pepper to taste

Wash and boil rice in 3 quarts of salted water for about 25 minutes or until soft. Drain and cool. Beat eggs lightly; add to rice. Add cheese and parsley; mix thoroughly. Roll into small balls (about size of walnut); dip in bread crumbs; fry in deep hot oil about 3 minutes or until golden brown. May be served as side dish with meat or fowl.

Serve hot. Serves 6.


## RISOTTO MILANESE

### RICE MILANESE

| | |
|---|---|
| 2 cups rice | ½ lb. chopped chicken |
| 1 large onion, sliced | giblets |
| 4 ozs. grated Parmesan | ¼ lb. butter |
| cheese | ½ tsp. saffron |
| 2 qts. chicken broth | Salt and pepper to taste |

Cook giblets in pint of boiling salted water about 20 minutes or until tender. Remove; chop into small pieces.

Melt butter in large pot; fry onion over low flame about 5 minutes or until brown. Remove onion. Add cleaned, washed rice and stir for 5 minutes to prevent burning. Then add 1 cup of broth; stir constantly.

Dissolve saffron in ½ cup of broth; allow to stand 5 minutes. Then strain saffron; add colored broth to rice. Stir well. Gradually add remainder of broth as the rice absorbs it. When rice has cooked about ½ hour, add half the cheese and continue stirring.

Add giblets; stir constantly. Add additional cup of

broth if rice becomes too dry. Entire process takes about
45 minutes, and when done is moist and creamy. Add
balance of grated Parmesan cheese.

Serves 6 to 8.

## Other Luncheon Delicacies

### CROCHE DI LATTE

#### MILK CROQUETTES

| | |
|---|---|
| 1 pt. lukewarm milk | 1 cup grated Romano |
| 2 ozs. butter | cheese |
| 8 tbs. flour | 1 tsp. chopped parsley |
| 1 cup bread crumbs | 3 tbs. chopped cooked |
| 2 eggs | ham |
| 2 cups peanut oil | Salt and pepper to taste |

Dissolve butter in pan over low flame; add parsley.
Cook about 3 minutes or until soft; stir constantly. Add
flour slowly, stirring until it forms a soft ball. Add lukewarm milk slowly; stir constantly until mixture is a very
smooth paste. This takes about 10 minutes. Remove from
fire; add 1 egg, ham, and cheese; stir again.

Cool until firm by spreading out on large platter.

In the meantime, beat other egg thoroughly.

Take 1 heaping tablespoon of cooled mixture and roll
into balls or croquettes. Dip in flour, then in beaten egg,
and roll in bread crumbs. Fry in deep, very hot peanut
oil about 2 minutes or until golden brown. May be served
hot or cold. Serves 6.

### FORMAGGIO CON OLIVE
### ALL'ARGENTIERA

#### CHEESE WITH OLIVES ARGENTIERA

| | |
|---|---|
| ½ lb. Italian black olives | ¼ lb. Incanestrato cheese |
| ¼ cup wine vinegar | 3 tbs. olive oil |

Cut cheese into 1-inch cubes. Heat oil in frying pan; add cheese and olives. Heat thoroughly over low flame about 15 minutes. Stir. Cheese grows slightly brown, does not melt. Add vinegar; boil up rapidly for 1 minute.

Serve very hot on toast. Serves 2 to 3.

## FRITTELLE DI PATATE

### POTATO PANCAKES

| | |
|---|---|
| 1½ lbs. potatoes | 1 small onion, chopped |
| 3 eggs | ¼ cup grated Pecorino |
| 1 tbs. chopped parsley | cheese |
| 1 cup peanut oil | 2 tbs. milk, if needed |
| 1¼ cups bread crumbs | Salt and pepper to taste |

Boil and mash potatoes; cool. Place in deep mixing bowl. Beat eggs well; add to potatoes. Stir into mixture onion, cheese, parsley, ½ cup of bread crumbs, salt and pepper to taste. If too dry, add enough milk for easy molding.

Mold mixture into cakes about 2½ inches in diameter and ½ inch thick. Dip in balance of bread crumbs. Fry in hot oil about 5 minutes or until golden brown on both sides.

Serve very hot. Serves 4 to 6.

## GUASTELLE CON FORMAGGIO

### SICILIAN ROLLS WITH CHEESE

| | |
|---|---|
| 6 Sicilian rolls | ½ lb. ricotta (Italian |
| ½ lb. Provolone cheese | cottage cheese) |
| 6 tsp. olive oil | Salt and pepper to taste |

Heat olive oil in small frying pan. Slice Provolone thin, about size of roll. Heat rolls in very hot oven 5 minutes to soften. Cut open through center.

Divide ricotta into 6 parts.

Pour 1 teaspoon of hot oil on one half of roll. Place slice of Provolone on it, then spread with portion of ricotta, a pinch of salt and pepper. Top with other half of roll and return to hot oven for 3 minutes. This forms a substantial sandwich.

Serve very hot. Serves 6.

## GUASTELLE CON SALSICCIA

### SICILIAN ROLLS WITH SAUSAGE

6 Sicilian rolls
6 links Italian sausage
3 large firm green
  peppers

6 tsp. olive oil
6 tbs. grated Romano
  cheese
Salt to taste

Broil sausage in very hot oven about 20 minutes or until golden brown and well done.

Cut peppers in half, take out seeds; broil in hot oven about 10 minutes or until light brown and tender. When cool, remove skins, if desired. Sprinkle with little salt.

Heat oil in frying pan. Heat rolls in very hot oven about 5 minutes to soften. Then cut open through center.

Place broiled sausage on roll; cover with broiled pepper; sprinkle lightly with grated cheese; pour 1 teaspoon of hot oil over all; cover with other half of roll. Return to oven for 3 minutes.

Serve very hot. Serves 6.

## PATATE CON OLIVE

### POTATOES WITH OLIVES

2 lbs. potatoes
3 tbs. butter
3 tbs. olive oil

1/4 lb. black Italian olives
1 sliced onion
Salt and pepper to taste

Peel potatoes and slice thinly.

Melt butter in large frying pan; add oil; heat. Add sliced potatoes. Fry over high flame for 10 minutes; stir frequently to prevent sticking. Lower flame; add sliced onion; cook for about 20 minutes or until potatoes are done. Add salt and pepper, olives; stir; cook 5 minutes longer.

Serve hot. Serves 4 to 6.

## POLENTA CON SALSICCIA

### CORN MEAL WITH SAUSAGE

2 cups corn meal
6 cups water
1 tsp. salt
2 tbs. olive oil
1 clove garlic
1 lb. Italian sausage

2 tbs. chopped parsley
2 tbs. butter
1 No. 2 can plum
  tomatoes
2 ozs. grated Parmesan
  cheese

Salt and pepper to taste

Place water in top part of large double boiler and boil.
As water bubbles rapidly, add salt. Gradually pour corn
meal into water, stirring constantly to prevent lumping.
Place boiling water in lower part of double boiler. Replace top of double boiler which contains corn-meal mixture. Cook slowly for 1 hour; stir frequently to insure
creamy consistency.

Cut sausage into small serving pieces; fry in hot oil for
15 minutes. Add all ingredients except cheese; cover; cook
over low flame about 1 hour.

To serve, spread half of hot corn meal on a very hot
platter; cover with half of sauce. Place balance of corn
meal on top; pour balance of sauce over this. Sprinkle
generously with grated Parmesan cheese.

Serve very hot. Serves 6 to 8.


## PIZZA SICILIANA

### SICILIAN TOMATO PIE

1 lb. flour
1 tsp. salt
1 cup lukewarm water
8 anchovy filets
1 cake yeast

2 tbs. peanut or olive oil
2 cups Plain Tomato
  Sauce #2
½ cup grated Pecorino
  cheese

Dissolve yeast in lukewarm water. Place sifted flour and
salt on board; add dissolved yeast. Knead thoroughly for

15 minutes. Add oil; continue kneading until smooth ball is obtained. Cover well. Set aside in warm place about 3 hours or until dough has raised to double its size.

In the meantime, prepare Plain Tomato Sauce #2. Cut anchovies into small pieces; add to sauce when done.

When dough has raised, spread in large well-greased baking pan about ½ to ¾ inches thick. Dent here and there with finger tips. Pour generous layer of sauce over dough; sprinkle liberally with grated Pecorino cheese. Bake in hot oven for ½ hour. Lower heat; continue baking for 15 minutes or until *pizza* is golden brown.

Remove from oven; cut into pieces about 4 to 5 inches square. Serve very hot. Serves 4 to 6.

## PIZZA CON SALSICCIA

### PIZZA WITH SAUSAGE

Follow same recipe and quantities as for Pizza Siciliana. Add ½ pound of Italian sausage cut into small pieces; arrange on dough *before* putting on the sauce and cheese. Bake as for Pizza Siciliana.

## PISELLI CON UOVA #1

### PEAS WITH EGGS #1

| | |
|---|---|
| 2 lbs. fresh peas | ¼ cup olive oil |
| 6 hard-boiled eggs | 1 cup hot water |
| 2 sliced onions | Salt and pepper to taste |

Shell peas. Heat half of oil in saucepan and cook onion about 5 minutes over slow flame or until soft. Add peas, ½ cup of water, salt, and pepper. Simmer; stir. As water is absorbed, gradually add more until peas are tender. This takes about 20 minutes.

Cut hard-boiled eggs in half lengthwise. Fry in balance of oil about 2 minutes or until slightly brown.

Place peas on hot serving dish and top with eggs.

Serve hot. Serves 4.

## PISELLI CON UOVA #2

### PEAS WITH EGGS #2

6 eggs
4 tbs. olive oil
1 large onion, chopped

1 No. 2 can tomatoes
1 can peas
Salt and pepper to taste

Heat oil in large shallow saucepan; add onion; cook about 2 minutes or until soft. Add tomatoes; simmer about 15 minutes. Add peas, salt, and pepper; simmer 10 minutes. Drop eggs in sauce one at a time. Be careful not to break yolks. Cook slowly about 3 minutes or until eggs are done.
Serves 6.

## SUFFLE DI VERMICELLI E POMODORO

### TOMATO-VERMICELLI SOUFFLÉ

1 cup canned tomatoes
3 tbs. olive oil
2 ozs. grated Parmesan
  cheese

½ lb. vermicelli
3 eggs
2 tbs. flour
Salt and pepper to taste

Heat oil over low flame in deep saucepan. Gradually stir in flour until well blended. Add tomatoes slowly; keep stirring. Bring to a boil; lower flame; simmer for 2 minutes. Add grated cheese, salt and pepper to taste; stir; turn off fire.
Break vermicelli into 1-inch pieces. Cook in 2 quarts of rapidly boiling salted water, about 6 minutes or until soft. Drain. Stir vermicelli into prepared sauce.
Beat egg yolks thoroughly; add. Beat egg whites stiff; fold in.
Transfer to buttered baking dish; bake in moderate oven about 10 minutes or until firm.
Serve hot. Serves 4.

# CHAPTER FOURTEEN

# Glossary of Italian Terms

| | |
|---|---|
| *Abbrustolito* | Toasted |
| *Acciughe* | Anchovy filets |
| *Acini di pepe* | Pasta; pepper-kernel type |
| *Affogati* | Steamed |
| *Agliata* | With garlic |
| *Aglio* | Garlic |
| *Agnellino* | Baby lamb |
| *Agro e dolce* | Sour and sweet |
| *Al; all'; alla* | As; in the style of |
| *Al burro* | Buttered |
| *Al dente* | Medium-cooked |
| *Al forno* | Baked; roasted |
| *All'aceto* | In vinegar |
| *Alla griglia* | Broiled |
| *All'olio* | In oil |
| *Amaretti* | Macaroons |
| *Aneto* | Dill |
| *Anguille* | Eels |
| *Anice* | Anise seed |
| *Anitra* | Duck |
| *Antipasto* | Hors d'oeuvres |
| *Aragosta* | Lobster |
| *Aranci* | Oranges |
| *Arancini* | Croquettes |
| *Aringhe* | Herring |
| *Arrostiti* | Roasted |
| *Asti Spumanti* | Italian champagne |
| *Autunno* | Autumn |
| | |
| *Baccalà* | Dry cod |
| *Bagaria* | Sicilian village |
| *Basilico* | Basil leaf |
| *Battesimo* | Christening |
| *Beccafico* | Stuffed (Sicilian dialect) |
| *Bel Paese* | Brand name for mild cheese |

| | |
|---|---|
| *Biscotti* | Cookies; biscuits |
| *Bistecca* | Beefsteak |
| *Bollito; bolliti* | Boiled |
| *Braciuolini* | Rollettes |
| *Broccoli* | Broccoli |
| *Brodo* | Broth |
| *Buon* | Good |
| *Buon Capo d'Anno* | Happy New Year |
| *Burro* | Butter |
| | |
| *Caciocavallo* | Hard Sicilian cheese |
| *Caffe espresso* | Black coffee |
| *Caffetiera* | Coffee maker |
| *Calamai* | Squids (fish) |
| *Cannella* | Cinnamon |
| *Capitone* | Large eel |
| *Capocollo* | Smoked pork |
| *Capo d'Anno* | New Year |
| *Cappelletti* | "Little Hats"; moist pasta |
| *Capperi* | Capers |
| *Carciofi* | Artichokes |
| *Carciofini* | Artichoke hearts |
| *Carne* | Meat |
| *Carnevale* | Carnival |
| *Cassata* | Cream tart |
| *Cassatelle* | Cream tartlets |
| *Cavatoni rigati* | Pasta; ribbed curved type |
| *Cavolfiore* | Cauliflower |
| *Cavolo* | Cabbage |
| *Cervelli* | Brains |
| *Cervo* | Venison |
| *Chianti* | Dry table wine; white or red |
| *Chiodo di garofini* | Cloves |
| *Cicoria* | Dandelion |
| *Cipolla* | Onion |
| *Colla; coll'* | With |
| *Compleanno* | Birthday |
| *Con* | With; and |
| *Con carne* | With meat |
| *Conchiglie* | Pasta; sea-shell type |
| *Coniglio* | Rabbit |

| | |
|---|---|
| Costatelle | Chops |
| Costatelle di vitella | Veal chops |
| Cotolette | Cutlets |
| Cresima | Confirmation |
| Croche | Croquettes |
| Cucuzza | Light green Italian squash |
| | |
| Di; d' | Of |
| Ditali | Pasta; short tubular type |
| Ditalini | Pasta; very short tubular type |
| Dolce | Sweet; sweetened; sweets |
| Dolci | Sweet; sweets |
| | |
| E | And |
| Escarola | Escarole |
| Estate | Summer |
| | |
| Fagiano | Pheasant |
| Fagioli | Beans |
| Fagiolini | String beans |
| Farfallette | Pasta; butterfly or bow-knot type |
| Fava | Fresh green bean; also dried |
| Fegatini | Chicken livers |
| Fegato | Liver |
| Festa | Holiday |
| Festa di San Giuseppe | St. Joseph's Day |
| Feste | Holidays |
| Feste invernale | Winter holidays |
| Fetucci | Pasta; bowknot type |
| Filetti | Filets |
| Filetto | Filet mignon |
| Fina | Fine; small |
| Finocchio | Anise-flavored Italian celery |
| Fiorentina | Florentine style |
| Foglie di alloro | Bay leaves |
| Formaggio | Cheese |
| Forno | Oven |
| Frittata | Omelet |

| | |
|---|---|
| *Frittelle* | Pancakes |
| *Fritto; fritti* | Fried |
| *Funghi* | Mushrooms |
| *Fusilli* | Pasta; curly spaghetti type |
| | |
| *Gamberi* | Shrimps |
| *Giuseppe* | Joseph |
| *Gnocchi* | Dumplings |
| *Gorgonzola* | Cheese; Roquefort type |
| *Griglia* | Broiled; a grill |
| *Guastelle* | Sicilian rolls |
| | |
| *Imbottiti; imbottite* | Stuffed |
| *Incanestrato* | Sicilian grating cheese |
| *Inglese* | English |
| *Insalata* | Salad |
| *Inverno* | Winter |
| | |
| *Lasagne* | Wide noodles |
| *Latte* | Milk |
| *Lattuga Romana* | Romaine (lettuce) |
| *Lesso* | Boiled |
| *Linguini* | Narrow noodles |
| *Lumache* | Snails |
| | |
| *Mafalde* | Pasta; twisted noodles |
| *Maggiorana* | Marjoram |
| *Maiale* | Pork |
| *Mandorla* | Almond |
| *Manteca* | Cheese and butter combined |
| *Manzo* | Beef |
| *Marinara* | Mariner style |
| *Marineo* | Sicilian village near Palermo |
| *Marsala* | Heavy sweet sherry |
| *Melenzana* | Eggplant |
| *Menta* | Mint |
| *Merluzzo* | Whiting |
| *Mezzani* | Pasta; curved type |
| *Milanese* | Milan style |
| *Minestra* | Thick vegetable soup |

| | |
|---|---|
| *Minestrone* | Thick soup |
| *Mostaccioli* | Pasta; oblique hollow type |
| *Mozzarella* | Moist unsalted cheese |
| *Mozzarella affumicata* | Smoked Mozzarella |
| | |
| *Natale* | Christmas |
| *Noce Moscata* | Nutmeg |
| *Nonni* | Grandmother |
| *Notte di Capo d'Anno* | New Year's Eve |
| | |
| *Olio* | Oil |
| *Olio d'oliva* | Olive oil |
| *Olive* | Olives |
| *Olive nere* | Black olives |
| *Olive nere all'olio* | Black olives in oil |
| *Oregano* | Herb; orégano; more delicate than thyme |
| *Oreganato* | With orégano |
| *Ossi buchi* | Veal shanks |
| *Ostriche* | Oysters |
| | |
| *Palermitana* | Palermo style |
| *Pane* | Bread |
| *Pane abbrustolito* | Toast |
| *Parmigiano* | Parmesan cheese |
| *Pasta* | Paste; dough; macaroni |
| *Pasticcio* | Pastry; piecrust |
| *Pastina* | Pasta; tiny disk type |
| *Pastina al uovo* | Pasta; made with egg |
| *Patate* | Potatoes |
| *Pecorino* | Goat's-milk cheese |
| *Pepe forte* | Crushed red pepper seeds |
| *Peperoni* | Green peppers |
| *Peperoncini* | Small peppers |
| *Peperoncini all'aceto* | Small green peppers in vinegar |
| *Perciatelli* | Pasta; long hollow type |
| *Pere* | Pears |
| *Pernice* | Partridge |
| *Pesca* | Peach |
| *Pesce* | Fish |
| *Pesche* | Peaches |

| | |
|---|---|
| *Pesciolini* | Minnows; tiny fish |
| *Piazza* | Public square |
| *Piccante* | Piquant |
| *Piccione* | Pigeon |
| *Pignoli* | Pine nuts |
| *Pimiento* | Sweet red pepper |
| *Piselli* | Peas |
| *Pizza* | Pie |
| *Pizzaiola* | "Like a little pie" |
| *Polenta* | Yellow corn meal |
| *Pollo* | Chicken; fowl |
| *Polpette* | Meat balls |
| *Polpettini* | Small meat balls |
| *Polpettone* | Meat loaf |
| *Pomodoro* | Tomato |
| *Prezzemolo* | Parsley |
| *Primavera* | Springtime |
| *Prosciutto* | Italian ham |
| *Provolone* | Mild slicing cheese |
| | |
| *Quaglia* | Quail |
| | |
| *Radici* | Radishes |
| *Ravioli* | Moist stuffed pasta |
| *Ricotta* | Italian cottage cheese |
| *Ricotta salata* | Very dry ricotta |
| *Rigatoni* | Pasta; large ribbed type |
| *Ripieno* | Stuffed; filled; stuffing |
| *Riso* | Rice |
| *Rognoni* | Kidneys |
| *Rollini* | Rollettes |
| *Romano* | Romano style |
| *Romano* | Tangy grating cheese |
| *Rosamarina* | Herb; rosemary |
| *Rosso* | Red |
| | |
| *Salami* | Smoked Italian sausage |
| *Salmone* | Salmon |
| *Salsa* | Sauce |
| *Salsa semplice* | Plain sauce |
| *Salsiccia* | Sausage |
| *Salsiccia con peperoni* | Sausage with peppers; hot sausage |

| | |
|---|---|
| *Salsiccia secca* | Very dry pork sausage |
| *Salute!* | Greetings! (a toast) |
| *Salvia* | Herb; sage |
| *San Giuseppe* | St. Joseph |
| *Sarde* | Sardines |
| *Savoiardi* | Lady fingers |
| *Scaloppine* | Thin veal cutlets |
| *Scamozza* | Pear-shaped cheese |
| *Scappati* | Fleeting; like a bird |
| *Sciacca* | Sicilian fishing village |
| *Sedani* | Celery hearts |
| *Selvaggio* | Wild |
| *Semplice* | Plain; simple |
| *Sfinge* | Cream puffs |
| *Sgombro* | Mackerel |
| *Siciliana* | Sicilian style |
| *Sogliole* | Sole |
| *Spada* | Swordfish |
| *Spaghetti* | Pasta; thin type |
| *Spaghettini* | Pasta; very thin type |
| *Sparagi* | Asparagus |
| *Spiedini* | Skewered; meat rolls on skewers |
| *Spinaci* | Spinach |
| *Spinola* | Striped bass |
| *Sposalizio* | Wedding |
| *Spumoni* | Italian ice cream |
| *Stocco* | Stockfish |
| *Strachino* | Tangy goat's-milk cheese |
| *Strufoli* | Clusters |
| *Suffle* | Soufflé |
| *Tagliarini* | Pasta; very narrow egg noodles |
| *Tartufata* | Truffle |
| *Timo* | Thyme |
| *Tonno* | Tuna fish |
| *Torta* | Tart; pie |
| *Trippa* | Tripe |
| *Trota* | Trout |
| *Tubettini* | Pasta; tiny tubular type |

| *Uccelli scappati* | Veal birds (northern Italian dialect) |
| *Umido* | Stew |
| *Uova* | Eggs |
| *Uovo* | Egg |
| *Uovo di aringhe* | Herring roe |
| *Uovo di tonno* | Tuna-fish roe |
| | |
| *Vermicelli* | Pasta; very thin type |
| *Vigilia di Natale* | Christmas Eve |
| *Vitella* | Veal |
| *Vongoli* | Clams |
| | |
| *Zafferano* | Herb; saffron |
| *Zia* | Aunt |
| *Zio* | Uncle |
| *Ziti* | Pasta; tubular type |
| *Zucchini* | Italian squash |
| *Zuppa* | Soup |

## Standard Measurements

| | |
|---|---|
| 2 cups butter or shortening | 1 lb. |
| 4 cups flour | 1 lb. |
| 2 cups sugar (granulated) | 1 lb. |
| 2 cups rice | 1 lb. |
| 2 cups | 1 pt. |
| 4 cups | 1 qt. |
| 4 qts. | 1 gal. |
| 4 tbs. flour | 1 oz. |
| 2 level tbs. butter or shortening | 1 oz. |
| 4 tbs. | ¼ cup |
| 16 tbs. | 1 cup |
| 3 tsp. liquid | 1 tbs. |
| 2 tbs. liquid | 1 oz. |
| 16 ozs. solids | 1 lb. |
| 16 ozs. liquid | 1 pt. |
| 25 drops of thin liquid | 1 tsp. |

*All measurements are level*

*Index*

# Index